V O L K S W A G E N
BEETLE
Coachbuilts and Cabriolets
1940 - 1960

TO THOSE WHO SOUGHT TO IMPROVE
AND THOSE WHO SEEK TO PRESERVE

VOLKSWAGEN
BEETLE
Coachbuilts and Cabriolets
1940 - 1960

KEITH SEUME & BOB SHAILL

© Copyright 1993 by Bay View Books Ltd
Published 1993 by Bay View Books Ltd
13a Bridgeland Street, Bideford
Devon EX39 2QE

ISBN 1 870979 33 8
Printed in Hong Kong

Foreword

This book came about as the result of a very happy coincidence. I had already been discussing with Charles Herridge of Bay View Books the possibility of a book about cabriolet versions of the Beetle. Unknown to me, Bob Shaill had been gathering information with the aim of perhaps one day finding someone to compile it all to produce a book on special-bodied Volkswagens.

Following a photographic session during which Bob's beautiful Stoll coupé was recorded for posterity, mention was made of this possible book. A plot was hatched, and here, two years later, is the result.

Without Bob's incredible archive full of rare and largely unpublished material, and without a whole army of like-minded enthusiasts world-wide, this book could never have seen the light of day. And that would have been a tragic shame, for never before has any meaningful attempt been made to catalogue the many coachbuilt and cabriolet Volkswagen Beetles. These cars – many of them crude, home-built affairs – deserve to be immortalized, for they represent an important, and previously untold, part of the amazing story of the Beetle.

The biggest problem we had when compiling this book was one of time. Publishing deadlines seem so far off when you start, but have a habit of creeping up on you when you least expect it. So it was with us. As the day of reckoning approached, 'new' cars still appeared out of the mists of time. Perhaps we should start preparing for a second volume...

If anyone out there has any information on these, or any other similar Volkswagen-based vehicle, please don't keep it to yourself. Drop us a line.

Keith Seume
Crondall, Hampshire
May 1993

If you would like to keep up with the latest news from the world of vintage Volkswagens, contact

The International Vintage Volkswagen Magazine
Bob Shaill
194 Old Church Road
St Leonards-on-Sea
East Sussex TN38 9HD
England

Or

VolksWorld Magazine
Keith Seume
Link House
Dingwall Avenue
Croydon
Surrey CR9 2TA
England

The authors would like to thank the following people without whom this book would not have been possible:

Andy Luzzi (Switzerland)* Luc de Paepe and Ann Leurart (Belgium)* Paul J Craft (USA)* Hans Otto Neubauer (Germany) Hans Joachim Klersy (Germany) Chris Barber (England) Alain Vuilleumier (Switzerland) Volkmar Kayser (Germany) Dr Philip Topcik (USA) Donald A Bartlett (USA) Blue Nelson (USA) Jacky Morel (France)* Barry Noble (Australia) Fred Metson (N. Ireland) Cliff Sedgman (Australia)* Milan Bumba (Czechoslovakia)* Martin Southwell (England)* Guenter Draude (Australia) Frans Raets (Belgium) Richard Cotton (England) Andy Holmes (England) Derek Frow (England) Richard King (England) Mike Key (England) Norman Hodson (England) David Fetherston (USA) Ulf Kaijser (Sweden) Annie Smith (France) Willi Kuhn (Switzerland) Jacques Ladyjensky (Belgium) Raoul Thiebaut (Belgium) Mr Cryns (Belgium) Autoworld Museum (Belgium) Dr B Wiersch (Wolfsburg Museum) FEBIAC (Belgium) Het Nieuwblad (Belgium) Yan Rami (England) Dr David Blight (England) and Major Ivan Hirst (England)

(*IVVM Correspondents)

The authors also wish to express their sincere thanks to Gwynn, Helene, Carrina and Judy for their never-ending support and understanding.

CONTENTS

INTRODUCTION
WHOEVER WOULD HAVE BELIEVED IT?

The Volkswagen Beetle is, without doubt, the most versatile car ever designed. How many other vehicles have been seen as a family saloon, a stylish two-seat roadster, an ambulance, a sportscar, a pick-up, a taxicab or a substitute for a fork lift truck?

These are just some of the rôles in which the Volkswagen Beetle – or its chassis – has found itself over the years. In addition, the Beetle was instrumental in the development of the wartime Type 82 Kübelwagen which provided mass transport for the Wehrmacht during World War II.

Even without such a show of versatility, the Beetle was destined for a place in automobile folklore. How many other vehicles can lay claim to having been designed by Ferdinand Porsche, funded by Adolf Hitler's Nazi party and ultimately rescued from almost certain oblivion by the British Army?

What is amazing is the incredible number of coachbuilding concerns across Europe which adopted the Beetle. Hungry for work in a deflated post-war economy, these coachbuilders – or *Karosseries*, to give them their German name – were responsible for producing some most intriguing vehicles.

At one end of the scale were companies such as Karmann and Hebmüller, who were responsible for building cabriolet and roadster models with official Wolfsburg factory support, while at the other were firms like Dannenhauer & Stauss, which built relatively few cars, each privately funded.

Alongside these were the many hundreds of one-off variations that ranged from professionally-styled and well-constructed coupés by leading design houses, to crude, home-built sports cars built from the remains of long-abandoned wartime Kübelwagens. Between these extremes lay a multitude of designs that were as exciting as they were unique.

In addition, the Beetle soon became the focus of attention from companies anxious to produced practical vehicles for a working population that was slowly recovering from the effects of a long and devastating war. Pick-ups, delivery vans, postal vehicles – all came to be produced using the humble Beetle as a starting point.

But why was there such an apparently large industry committed to using the Volkswagen as a base vehicle? The truth is that the industry was not particularly large. In real terms, the total number of people employed in the post-war coachbuilding industry in Europe could be counted in the low thousands.

However, what is important to appreciate is that although there were relatively few people employed in the *Karosseries*, the contribution they made towards helping to get a war-torn Europe back on its feet was great. Remember, there were few factories left standing capable of building a vehicle from scratch, and what vehicles had survived the war were by and large worn out and beyond repair. This situation was immediately recognized by the occupying forces in Germany, and representatives of the British Army – notably Colonel Michael McEvoy and Major Ivan Hirst – sought to restart production of the Volkswagen at the Wolfsburg plant in 1945.

Within a few months of the end of hostilities, the first Beetles began to appear on the roads of Germany, driven, for the most part, by military personnel of varying nationalities. It was only a matter of time before representatives of some of the established coachbuilders in Germany, among them Wilhelm Karmann and Joseph Hebmüller, approached the factory to seek commissions, or to purchase cars for their own projects.

There were few alternatives to the Volkswagen but, fortunately, with its self-contained chassis and drive-train it proved to be an excellent starting point. The greatest problem in these early years – and indeed, it has to be said, for many years to come – was the reluctance of the factory to sell bare chassis to anyone who did not benefit from the factory seal of approval.

The consequent shortage of available chassis did

Ferdinand Porsche, seen to the left of the windscreen, shows an interested Hermann Goering an early prototype KdF cabriolet. Nazi Party officials make a show of sharing Goering's enthusiasm.

From the very beginning a cabriolet version of the Beetle was considered. This 1938 model looks little different from the post-war cabriolets built by Karmann.

little to deter work-hungry coachbuilders, for there were abandoned military vehicles spread liberally across Europe and North Africa ripe for the picking. Stripped of their utilitarian bodyshells, these provided a useful source of Volkswagen chassis for *Karosserie* and enthusiast alike. It is particularly interesting to discover that many special-bodied Volkswagens were built in Czechoslovakia, where derelict Kübelwagens were

plentiful in the immediate post-war period.

There was no shortage of clients for the coach-builders either, for as currency reform began to take its effect across Germany, a demand for 'interesting' cars began to blossom. After all, this was a country with a history of coachbuilding where, prior to the war, it was commonplace for a customer to order a bare chassis and arrange for its delivery to a favoured coach-

Even the factory tried its hand at building the occasional special Beetle to order. This car was built for the Emperor of Abyssinia. Note the steering wheel – evidently the Emperor was a large man requiring more leg room! The trim is very lavish compared with the austere upholstery of normal Beetles. The hubcaps were interesting too, of a design only used once more, on Hebmüller No.2.

works. There, the customer would discuss his or her particular needs and preferences, whereupon the coachbuilder would design and construct a one-off body to suit.

Even the Volkswagen factory exploited the demand, with at least one specially-trimmed Beetle being built, for the Emperor of Abyssinia. With extra trim and leopardskin upholstery, the Emperor's Beetle was very lavish in its appearance.

Today, there is little need for such an industry, for there is a wide variety of vehicles of every conceivable style on offer in showrooms across Europe. Also, with the high cost of labour today, any private commission would be an extremely expensive proposition, putting the prospect of a coachbuilt special far out of reach of the ordinary man.

This book can by no means be considered as a definitive listing of every special-bodied Volkswagen

Beetle ever built, for the simple reason that new discoveries are being made all the time. Hopefully, its publication will help to prise yet more coachbuilts and cabrios out of the barns and workshops where they are no doubt hiding.

And why cover the years 1940 to 1960? Simply because prior to the earlier date there was little in the way of activity on the coachbuilding front as far as Volkswagens are concerned. It also marks the introduction of the Type 82 Kübelwagen, which lent its chassis to so many early specials. The year 1960 marks the start of the 'beach buggy' era, with the widespread use of glassfibre as a body-making material, and the beginning of the end of the age of coachbuilding.

Before any attempt can be made to catalogue the many variations on the Beetle theme, it is important to take a fresh look at the history that lies behind this versatile little car. It is a remarkable tale.

Volkswagen saw its Karmann cabriolet as representing all that was great about post-war Germany. Early Reutters advertising artwork shouted the message loud and clear.

One of the most celebrated conversions of all was that carried out by Joseph Hebmüller, turning a regular Beetle saloon into a very stylish roadster.

THE HISTORY
FROM THE ASHES OF WOLFSBURG

The story begins with a modest yet immensely talented engineer by the name of Ferdinand Porsche. Born on September 3rd, 1875, at Maffersdorf, Porsche was the son of a respected tinsmith. He joined his father as an apprentice, but had his sights set on greater things, and while attending evening classes at the technical college at nearby Reichensberg, he developed a lasting interest in two comparatively recent technological developments: domestic electricity and the internal combustion engine.

Porsche's first full-time job was with Bela Egger, an electrical company of which he became manager of the test department after just four years. His skills brought him to the attention of Jacob Lohner, a Viennese coachbuilder. Lohner gave Porsche his first opportunity to design an automobile, with electricity as the means of propulsion. However, unlike other machines which relied upon chains or belts to drive the wheels, Porsche's design featured motors fitted directly to the hub of each front wheel. Although it was without doubt technologically interesting – especially for 1900 – Porsche was not over-pleased with the car, considering it slow and too limited in range. However, further development resulted in a number of other designs, each more impressive than its predecessor. Eventually, Porsche's creations came to be used successfully in competition – a foretaste of things to come.

Following a period of military service, Porsche joined the Austro-Daimler company in 1905, remaining there until 1923. During his period with the company Ferdinand Porsche was responsible for some superb vehicles. In 1910, three cars were entered in the legendary seven-day Prince Henry Trial – they finished in first, second and third positions out of an entry of 176 cars. The winning vehicle was driven by Ferdinand Porsche himself.

He left Austro-Daimler a restless man, and joined Daimler for a period of five-and-a-half years in the position of technical director. During this period he was responsible for many of the classic Daimler designs, but he had aspirations of a very different kind, for he had become fascinated by the idea of a small car for the masses. He opened a design office in Stuttgart where he was able to work unhindered by the pressures of a large company, patenting his own design for suspension: the torsion bar. This was a significant development in the future history of the people's car – and, as far as Auto-Union racing cars were to be concerned, an important step on the path to victory.

Late in 1931, Porsche gathered his team together and began discussing his ideas for a popular car. Many others had tried to tackle the problem of how to design a car that could be built inexpensively, be easy to maintain and yet offer a level of comfort more often associated with larger vehicles. As far as Porsche was concerned, there was no need for cars to be so large. Most made poor use of available space by slavishly following the old, coachbuilder's ways: the carriage always follows the horse. In automobile terms this could be translated as a front-mounted engine pulling the car along behind.

With the memory of his hub-driven Lohner design still fresh in his mind, Porsche began to look at alternatives to the conventional layout. By placing the engine at the rear, better use could be made of internal space, with overall size being consequently reduced. If a vehicle could be made smaller then there would be no need for a heavy chassis, and by using the body of the car itself to add stiffness to the design, then the weight could be further reduced. He recognized that any successful small vehicle had to benefit from independent suspension front and rear, and began to develop his idea of using torsion bars as a springing medium. These simple devices appeared to offer the perfect solution to the problem of ride quality being progressive in action – the more they are deformed, the stiffer they become.

In 1931, Porsche penned Project No 12 – a small car that incorporated many of his ideas. It was a four-

Prototypes V1 (saloon) and V2 (cabriolet) were extensively road-tested during 1936 and are seen here with Ferry and Ferdinand Porsche.

Conceived in 1931, Porsche Project 12 was built in prototype form by Zündapp but was shelved when Zündapp returned to building motorcycles.

wheeled vehicle with rear-mounted air-cooled engine and fully independent suspension. It could seat four people in comfort and came with a luggage compart-ment in front of the driver. Only Dr Fritz Neumeyer of the Zündapp motorcycle company recognized the potential offered by Porsche's design as he too had been considering the viability of a *Volksauto* – a car for the person that today could afford a motorcycle, but tomorrow may buy a car. Together, Zündapp and Porsche built their first prototype people's car. The only significant change to Project No 12 was the use of a five-cylinder water-cooled radial engine in place of the three-cylinder air-cooled design favoured by Porsche. The results were disastrous, as early testing of

three prototypes showed that the engines were flawed from the outset. Two seized within a few miles. Further development gradually solved these early problems, but by the end of 1932 the motorcycle was experiencing renewed interest, so Zündapp took the opportunity to pull out of the venture.

At about this time Porsche received an offer from the Russian government to visit their country with a view to working there on the development of future automobile projects. Although impressed with what he saw, Porsche the family man could not bring himself to move to Russia.

Towards the end of 1932, the NSU factory met with Porsche to consider the production of another *Volksauto* design similar to that of Zündapp. Porsche readily agreed to the project but suggested that this time the engine should be cooled by air, and of horizontally-opposed design. The result was another beetle-like vehicle but with improved lines and a reduced weight. Testing showed that the car, designated Type 32, had a relatively high top speed – approximately 55mph – and excellent reliability, unlike its Zündapp predecessors, but unfortunately an agreement with Italian car makers FIAT, dating back several years, forbade NSU to manufacture cars, so reluctantly the idea was shelved once again.

By now, an ambitious political figurehead named Adolf Hitler was showing not inconsiderable interest in the affairs of Porsche. His first introduction to Porsche was as a result of discussions over the Porsche-designed Auto Union racing car. The meeting left Hitler impressed by the engineer.

When Hitler's great plans for the future of Germany included a 'People's Car', he turned to the motor industry for designs that would fulfil a number of criteria: the vehicle had to be capable of a sustained speed of 100kmh (approximately 62mph); it must record fuel consumption figures of no worse than 7 litres per 100km (or 40mpg); it must be able to carry four passengers in comfort so that parents and children could travel together; the engine should be air-cooled to cope with the harsh German winters; finally, the cost must be no more than 1000 Reich Marks (RM 1000 – equivalent to about $250, or £50, at the time!). Porsche's designs fitted the bill perfectly but for one thing: price. His idea of a *Volksauto*, or *Volks-Wagen*, would cost closer to RM 2800, and despite discussions with Hitler, Porsche could not dissuade him from the dream of the thousand Mark car. To Porsche it was both madness – and a challenge. Although he genuinely doubted that such a car could be built at the price, he began work on the final designs. Members of the German automobile industry were involved in the project, with Daimler-Benz called upon to price the chassis, Ambi-Budd (the famous Berlin bodyworks which was part-American owned) to look at the bodyshell, and Adler to weigh up the likely cost of production.

To Porsche, the go-ahead effectively meant picking up where he had left off with the old NSU Type 32. The new vehicle was designated Type 60 and closely resembled the earlier design except in the engine department, where Porsche ultimately settled on an air-cooled flat-four designed by Franz

A series of thirty cars –
titled VW30 – was built
in 1936/37. They were
powered by a 985cc
four-cylinder horizon-
tally-opposed air-cooled
engine.

The VW30s saw exten-
sive testing in the
hands of German
soldiers, who were
given instructions to
drive each car a
minimum of 80,000km.
The cars performed
well.

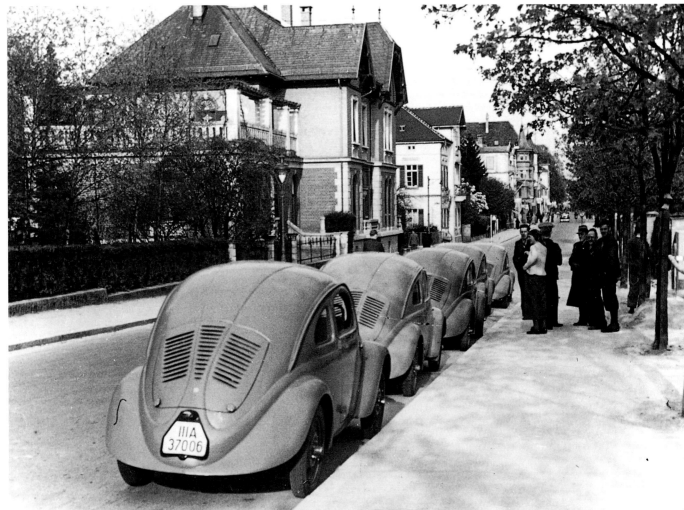

Reimspiess. Hitler made a fund available to build three prototypes of Porsche's new car in a scant ten-month period, supposedly with the help of other German car manufacturers, but that help was never forthcoming. Jealousy over Porsche's apparent favour with Hitler put paid to any assistance, and the three prototypes were assembled in Porsche's own garage in Stuttgart as there were no suitable facilities at his design offices.

By October 1936, two cars were ready for testing. They were a sedan (V1) and a cabriolet (V2) which shared much with the earlier designs for Zündapp and NSU, and which sowed the seeds for the car that is today so familiar on our roads. The body was a rounded, two-door design, while the chassis comprised a flat pan with a central backbone. At the front, a transverse torsion bar system formed the suspension. At the rear, suspension was once again by torsion bar, with the swing-axle design centring around a transaxle mounted between two forks on the chassis. The engine was a horizontally-opposed, four-cylinder, four-stroke, air-cooled unit of 995cc capacity.

Soon after, a further three cars – designated VW-Series 3 (VW3) – were completed, these being built by the Daimler Benz company. While from an aesthetic standpoint the VW3 vehicles were not a great success, the engines proved to be well able to withstand almost everything the official RDA (*Reichsverband der Deutschen Automobilindustrie*) testers could throw at them – that is, once the original fragile cast-iron crankshaft had been replaced by a steel forging.

By the end of 1937, the RDA published its report and presented it to Hitler. He decided that the project should now be funded by the German Labour Front (DAF – but not to be confused with the Dutch manufacturer of the same name), the replacement for the now banned trade unions. In reality this meant that the German workers were themselves funding the project, for the DAF's funds were nothing more than confiscated trade union monies topped up with compulsory 'donations' from the workers' wages.

Money was thus made available for the construction of another thirty prototypes – the Series 30, or VW30. By now, the design had been refined still further, with the body bearing a much closer resemblance to the final production version. However, the rear bodywork had been punched full of large louvres to aid cooling and to give the driver some rear vision.

As a final acid test of the VW30's capabilities, the RDA drafted in 200 soldiers to drive the cars at least 50,000 miles over a variety of terrain. The testing, overseen by Porsche himself, was a success and all that remained was to finalize the still awkward styling.

The date: 26th May 1938. The place: KdF-Stadt, later to become known simply as Wolfsburg – home of the Volkswagen. The official cornerstone laying ceremony.

In a still from a rare archive film, Hitler acknowledges the assembled crowds from the passenger seat of one of the earliest cabriolet versions.

In the end, relatively few alterations were made to the overall design, but they included changing the doors from rear-hinged suicide type to a more conventional and safer front-hinged style. At the rear of the car, a pair of windows were added, being symmetrical about a central bar, and the louvres in the engine cover were moved to the more familiar position under the rear windows.

Porsche made two trips to the USA to examine the mass-production techniques pioneered by Ford. He asked numerous questions, timed every step of the manufacturing process to the second and finally left convinced that if the Americans could do it, so could he.

When it came to the matter of putting the car into full production, various schemes were examined before Hitler decided that the only viable proposition was to build a factory from scratch. A search of the countryside for a suitable site – one that had ready access to a waterway and a main railway line – showed that the 14th-century estate of Count von Schulenburg, Schloss Wolfsburg, was ideal. Plans for the new plant were drawn up at Hitler's request by Peter Koller, a young architect, under the guidance of Robert Ley, chief of the Nazi Party Labour Organisation. Following Porsche's visit to the Ford assembly plant in Dearborn, the factory was to be modelled on the latest American facilities.

On May 26th, 1938, the cornerstone of the new factory was laid in a ceremony overseen by Adolf

First there was the KdF-Wagen, then the KdF-Stadt – and now here's the KdF home! The Kraft durch Freude movement had a vision of the future that saw every German living in a perfect house, driving his perfect car. The dream was short-lived.

Hitler himself. He announced that the new car would be called the *Kraft durch Freude* (Strength Through Joy) car – or KdF-Wagen – and the new town surrounding the factory, KdF-Stadt. With the most modern production equipment and a workforce including a number of repatriated, US-trained Germans, the scene was set for one of the greatest stories in automotive history, but the small matter of how the financially-deprived German people would be able to afford even a car as inexpensive as the KdF-Wagen still remained. A scheme that only a man like Hitler could dream up provided the 'solution'. The Nazi DAF organisation established a saving scheme whereby the average German worker could save for his car by purchasing a weekly RM5 savings stamp which was to be pasted into a KdF savings book.

Although at first sight this savings scheme seemed like a good idea, in reality it was little more than a way to raise money for the whole project ahead of actual production. The true cost of joining the scheme proved somewhat higher than the purchase price of a KdF-Wagen. The vehicle itself would cost RM 990, on top of which there was a RM 50 delivery charge, and another RM 200 for two years' compulsory insurance. At a time when the average working wage was RM 200-300 per month, the KdF-Wagen was not quite the bargain it first appeared to be, yet despite the inclusion of non-cancellation clauses and other dubious requirements, some 336,638 people signed up with the KdF-Wagen savings plan. Raising a total of RM 280 million between them, none ever came to own a car of his own under this scheme...

When, in 1939, war was declared in Europe, orders came from on high that Porsche should immediately design and build a military vehicle based on the KdF-Wagen. The suitability of the car for military use had not escaped the German army even before war broke out and, as early as 1938, prototype work had been carried out under Porsche's instructions. In 1940, however, the Type 82 finally arrived – a simple, slab-sided four-door body produced by Ambi-Budd mounted on a KdF-Wagen floorpan which was modified for increased ground clearance. The design became known as the Kübelwagen (literally translated as 'bucket car'). It became the mainstay of the German army throughout the war, performing much the same duties as the famed American General Purpose Vehicle, or Jeep, and despite being unable to match the minimum power output required of military vehicles (22.5bhp as opposed to a stipulated 25bhp), the Kübelwagen soldiered on largely unchanged until 1943, when at last a larger, more powerful engine of 1131cc capacity was introduced, giving a slightly healthier 25bhp.

There were numerous variations on the Kübelwagen theme, the best known being the amphibious Schwimmwagen. By the end of hostilities, some 50,000 Kübelwagens and 14,000 Schwimmwagens had been produced, along with a total of just 210 KdF-Wagens (none destined for public consumption, needless to say). There was also an assortment of KdF-Wagen variations which

Major Ivan Hirst, on the left, was largely responsible for getting the factory back on its feet. The trilby-hatted German is Hirst's secretary, Karl Schmücker.

included the Type 82E and the Type 87 – a KdF-Wagen body mounted on two- or four-wheel drive versions of the Kübelwagen chassis respectively.

When the war finally came to an end, the KdF-Stadt factory lay in ruins, the consequence of heavy Allied bombing. It was ultimately liberated by the Americans on 10-11th April, 1945. With the factory all but destroyed, a workforce (foreign forced labour and Russian prisoners of war) which had gone on the rampage and disappeared, and an acute shortage of all basic necessities, including food, things didn't look good for the future of the People's Car, but when the task of rebuilding the factory was assigned to Major Ivan Hirst of the Royal Electrical and Mechanical Engineers (REME), things began to look up.

Hirst arrived in Wolfsburg in August 1945 as a Military Government (MilGov) officer. There was already a British Army detachment there operating in one corner of the factory and supervising the overhaul of trucks formerly used by the German Army, prior to reissuing them to the German civilian population. It was considered vital to provide transportation again, as the railway system was still largely inoperative at this time. A few cars – Kübelwagens – had already been assembled from parts left over from the wartime programme, but any idea of real production was a MilGov responsibility, and Hirst was put in for that task. As the Volkswagen company had been wholly owned by the Nazi party – or rather the DAF – and as that had now been abolished by Allied decree, the

Wolfsburg factory now had no owner.

The idea of starting production of the Volkswagen once again so as to provide inexpensive transport for the Allied forces in Germany was the brainwave of Colonel Michael McEvoy. McEvoy, whose story is more fully told in Chapter Four, had long been involved with cars but at the end of the war he had the task of getting the German garage trade back into operation in the British zone of occupation. His responsibilities at army headquarters included the small detachment at Wolfsburg and he suggested that, by restarting production of the Volkswagen, the occupying forces could be provided with transport at no cost to the British taxpayer. The matter of light transportation was an important one, for all that was available to the British were wartime 15cwt trucks and light utilities that had all but reached the end of their useful lives.

At first progress was slow, with so much damage having been done by Allied air raids and with no labour force apart from the German supervisors who had stayed on at Wolfsburg. From the twisted debris of the shop floor, and from the wartime dispersal sites, what machinery remained was pressed into service to produce desperately-needed vehicles. One of the early KdF cars was painted khaki green and dispatched to the British Army headquarters. Immediately an order for 20,000 was on its way back to Hirst. The Americans decided they wanted some, as did the French and the Russians.

The simplest solution would have been to produce

19

Innenlenker mit Faltdach

Three versions of the KdF-Wagen were envisaged. The saloon and cabriolet models were designed alongside a sun-roof model (left) that featured a full-length canvas roof.

On the road to success – a scene from the 1951 Berlin Motor Show (right) with Volkswagens outnumbering everything in sight. In the background, a lone Porsche stands guard.

the Kübelwagen, but its body had been made at the now-destroyed Ambi-Budd factory in Berlin. It was therefore necessary to get the Wolfsburg press shop back in operation and to build new jigs for the assembly of the individual body panels.

Having regard to what was likely to be available, the top Germans immediately put in place a system of identifying the various vehicle types that could be produced: Type 1 was the KdF-Wagen saloon, the Kübelwagen became the Type 2 and the old Type 82 became the Type 5. Several variations of each were planned, including fire tenders, vans and pick-ups, but the lack of raw materials meant that it would be some while before such dreams could be realized.

Hirst had to set up a new German management comprising VW people who had successfully survived the 'De-Nazification' process instituted by the Allies, plus a few appointed from outside. A veritable game of musical chairs ensued: some men were dismissed as politically unacceptable and others reinstated following appeal, but eventually a fairly stable management was established. As for the production operatives and other 'blue-collar' workers, many were recruited among prisoners of war being released from camps in the British zone. They were housed in huts around the factory that had been put up for the wartime foreign workers and Russian PoWs.

Supervising the German management was the British board for the VW organization, i.e. for the factory and the town of Wolfsburg. This board functioned as a board of directors, with Colonel C R

Radclyffe at headquarters as its chairman on the industry side, and Ivan Hirst, along with a colleague on the financial side, as 'executive directors'. Hirst also had a deputy at Wolfsburg, and support from the Army who agreed to provide a quality-control back-up team. Ivan Hirst has often said that the re-establishment of Volkswagen after the war was a team effort, German and British: 'The Germans, at all levels, worked very hard, in deplorable conditions...'.

The factory had been listed as a potential 'war reparations' package – effectively payment for expenses incurred by Allied forces during the war – and several countries expressed an interest in acquiring the Volkswagen factory after the war. At first, Australia showed considerable enthusiasm, having little in the way of an engineering industry at that time. However, the MilGov had placed a four-year reserve on the factory as being essential to Allied occupation requirements. The Australians were not prepared to wait that long and lost interest. Ford was a possible taker, as the industry side of MilGov initially felt that the best solution would be for the factory to be taken over by an existing car manufacturer, and Ford, of course, already had a factory in Germany, at Cologne.

Hirst attended meetings of the motor industry association, feeling somewhat the odd man out in his British army uniform, and here he met two British representatives from the Ford works at Dagenham who were in charge of Cologne. They soon discovered that they had problems in common, not least being the supply of raw materials. This led to the offer

of a job with Ford at Dagenham, but Hirst declined, preferring to see MilGov's Volkswagen operation through to the end. In 1948 Henry Ford II visited the Cologne factory, where he met Colonel Radclyffe and talked about Wolfsburg, but when Ford learned that it was only a few kilometres from the Russian Zone boundary, he considered that it was too much of a political hot potato.

The British Rootes group, too, has been mentioned as a possible bidder for the factory. Soon after the end of hostilities, Sir William Rootes came to Wolfsburg looking for a machine to make press tools for large body panels, but it had been destroyed by the Allied bombing. Hirst showed him round the factory, or rather what was left of it at that time. Sir William viewed it with polite interest, but at the end of the tour turned to his host and said, 'Well it's been a nice day young man, but if you think you're going to get cars built here, you're a bloody fool!'.

Hirst explains that, just prior to the end of the war in Europe, arrangements had been made in Britain whereby representatives of the engineering industry would enter Germany after the end of hostilities and take a close look at German factories. The idea was to see what could be learned with a view to pursuing the war against Japan. Although Japan, too, was soon out of the war, the scheme continued and it seems that this is how two examples of the Volkswagen found themselves at the Humber factory, where they were stripped down and a report drawn up. Whoever had the task of tearing these cars apart must have been somewhat surprised to find the widespread use of light alloys in the power train, and independent suspension on all wheels. They concluded that the car had no economic future.

When full-scale production was on the horizon, Radclyffe and Hirst went to the 1947 International Motor show at Paris in order to establish the position of the Beetle on the open market. The car that seemed to be directly comparable was the Skoda, a rear-engined, water-cooled, small car that appeared to be well-designed and well-built. Today, the wheel has turned, and VW controls Skoda.

By the middle of 1947, the Allied requirement had been largely met, and the end of the four-year reserve period was in sight. Meanwhile, the political situation was changing dramatically, with the Russians isolating themselves more and more from the Allies. The Iron Curtain had fallen and life in certain parts of Europe would never be the same again. However, the feeling among those involved with Wolfsburg was that the Volkswagen had a future. With the agreement of his colleagues on the board, Hirst began to look for

someone – a German – to reinforce the factory management. By chance, he heard of a man by the name of Heinz Nordhoff, formerly of Opel, who was looking for a job. Under the rules applied by the Americans, he could not hold an executive position with any company in the US Zone because he had received an honorary title from the Nazi party during the war. However, the British rulings on such matters were different, so Hirst invited Nordhoff to Wolfsburg for a general talk.

Hirst interviewed him initially for the position of deputy, but after two days he became convinced that Nordhoff was the right man to take overall control at Wolfsburg. He was sent up to meet Radclyffe at head-quarters, who agreed with Hirst, and the MilGov board appointed Heinz Nordhoff as General Director of Volkswagen, starting from January 1st 1948.

Volkswagen exports had begun in 1947 to earn US dollars to offset the cost of food imports into Germany paid for by UK taxpayers. In mid-1948, the German currency reform took place and the general economy began to take off as a result. There was already a massive pent-up demand for the new Volkswagen from the German civilian population, as well as from neighbouring countries. By later in 1948, Wolfsburg was no longer on the reparations list, allowing Nordhoff virtual free rein to complete the final step of turning what had once been a war-torn, virtually derelict, ownerless car factory into a commercially-viable operation. Ivan Hirst had what he described as the uncomfortable job of sitting alongside Nordhoff for a further year-and-a-half as a safety net in case he fell down on the job; there need have been no concern. Finally, Radclyffe, as chairman of the British board, handed the company over to the German Minister of Economics late in 1949.

From this point on, Volkswagen was a car manu-facturer in its own right and at long last, after a wait of almost ten years, the Beetle finally became, in the truest sense, the people's car it was meant to be. Heinz Nordhoff remained the top man at Volkswagen until his death in 1968, having seen the company rise from the ashes of post-war Germany to become one of the largest car manufacturers in the world.

Sadly, Dr Porsche himself played no part in the rebirth of his beloved Volkswagen, having been imprisoned by the French on what are said to have been somewhat spurious charges. Subsequently suffering prolonged ill-health, he passed away on January 30th 1951 at the age of 75.

Without Porsche, Hirst and Nordhoff, the dream of a people's car would probably never have become a reality.

A FIRM FOUNDATION
THE VW CHASSIS AND ENGINE

There can be few chassis that lend themselves so readily to being fitted with a body other than that for which they were designed. However, the Volkswagen chassis, being a relatively self-contained design, offered the coachbuilder almost infinite possibilities. Designed at a time when the majority of production cars had a separate, girder-type chassis with a front-mounted, in-line engine and rear-wheel drive, the Volkswagen was unique. It had a rear-mounted, horizontally-opposed, air-cooled engine, driving through a transaxle, mounted in a chassis that consisted of little more than a central backbone and two pressed-steel floorpans. For suspension, whereas the average car had a live axle with cart springs at both ends, the Volkswagen sported four-wheel independent suspension with torsion bars.

The body of the Volkswagen, whether Beetle or Kübelwagen, was attached by a series of bolts around the periphery. Removing the body from the chassis was a relatively straightforward task and required only the most basic tools. To begin with, the battery and electrical systems are disconnected, followed by the fuel tank. The steering column is released from the steering box by undoing the flexible coupling, and then it is a case of removing the bolts that hold the body to the chassis. The majority of these – just under thirty or so in all – are located along the sills and under the rear seat area of the car. Once the bolts have been removed, the body may be lifted free from the chassis. Refitting the fuel tank and steering column would, if necessary, allow the chassis to be moved under its own power.

Few other vehicles were so conveniently designed from the coachbuilder's point of view, and in view of the fact that there were so many Volkswagen, especially Kübelwagen, chassis lying unused across Europe, it is easy to see why they became popular with so many coachbuilders in the immediate post-war period.

Looking at the chassis in detail, the front suspension consists of a pair of torsion bars running trans-

The chassis of a VW30 prototype clearly shows Porsche's torsion-bar suspension and central backbone. This early photograph has been printed back to front!

A rare photograph of a new KdF-Wagen chassis. Clearly seen is the ingenious torsion-bar suspension and the cylindrical fuel tank unique to the KdF-Wagen.

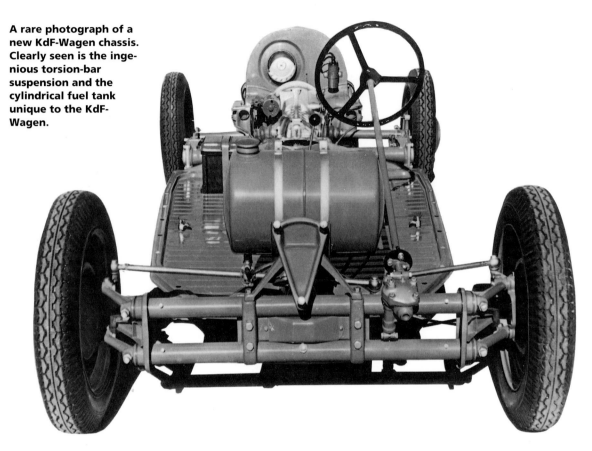

versely across the car. These are not the more common solid torsion bars, but multi-leaf bars which allow a softer spring rate with no loss of strength. They are housed in grease-filled tubes which are in turn bolted to the framehead of the chassis.

At the outer ends of the torsion bars are trailing arms and these connect via swivel – or link – pins to the spindle assemblies. Conventional kingpins allow the spindles to pivot for steering.

The steering box itself is bolted to the upper torsion bar tube, and is operated by a simple straight steering column that passes through the front bulkhead. A single flexible joint is incorporated in the column close to the steering box.

Unequal-length track rods connect to steering arms on the spindle assemblies at the outer end and to an asymmetrically-shaped drop arm on the steering box at the inner end. Rubber-cased ball-joints – with grease nipples on early versions – allow for suspension and steering movement.

This whole assembly bolts to the central backbone of the chassis, which runs from the front all the way through the inside of the car to just ahead of the transmission. The backbone is deep, providing considerable strength to what would otherwise be a very flexible chassis. Indeed, contrary to popular opinion, the

Volkswagen chassis relies heavily on the bodyshell to provide rigidity. This was discovered only too frequently by coachbuilders who sought to build cabriolet models by the simple expedient of slicing the roof off a Beetle saloon.

Quite apart from its task of giving strength to the chassis, the backbone also serves to house the control cables (clutch, accelerator, handbrake, choke), gear linkage and fuel line. The rear brake pipe runs, perhaps somewhat oddly, alongside the backbone.

At a point just ahead of the transmission, the backbone divides into two forks which pass either side of the gearbox and terminate alongside the clutch bellhousing. The rear transmission mountings attach to these forks at this point, while the front mounting is to be found where the backbone splits into two. The engine itself has no mountings as such, being simply bolted onto – and cantilevered off – the rear of the transmission casing.

The rear suspension is once again by transverse torsion bars, this time a pair of solid bars being used. The inner ends are located in splines in the backbone of the chassis, while the outer ends are supported in rubber bushings and are also splined to carry a pair of trailing arms.

These trailing arms connect with the outer ends of

The rear swing-axle suspension relies on a pair of transverse torsion bars and lever-arm dampers. Note how the engine is bolted to the light alloy transmission without any other form of support. Brakes were cable-operated on all early VWs.

the rear axle tubes in which the drive shafts are to be found. The inner ends of these tubes pivot at the transmission, making the suspension a swing-axle design. To allow for the fact that any swing axle suspension causes the outer ends of the axles to describe an arc, the trailing arms are made of spring steel and actually twist as the suspension moves up and down.

The biggest drawback of this suspension design is that there are constant changes in wheel camber angle – compressing the suspension gives negative camber, extending it, positive camber. The result of this is somewhat unstable handling on the limit of adhesion although, in the hands of a skilled driver, a Volkswagen could easily outcorner the vast majority of contemporary small saloon cars. Indeed, it is important to note that this suspension design is virtually identical to that used by Porsche – it was, of course, designed by Ferdinand Porsche – in the 356 models all the way up to the 1960s and the advent of the 911 range.

The main advantage of the torsion bar as a suspension medium is that it provides rising rate springing – the more the torsion bar is twisted, the stiffer it becomes. The torsion bar is also a very compact and relatively maintenance-free item. Single-action, lever-arm dampers were used at the rear up until 1951 when

conventional telescopic units were fitted, matching those used on the front suspension.

As far as the braking system is concerned, all early examples were equipped with cable-operated drum brakes. All Type 82 Kübelwagens were cable-braked, as were all Beetles until early in 1950. From then on, export (Deluxe) models came with four-wheel hydraulic brakes, but cable brakes remained on all 'standard' models until as late as 1962.

The transmission on all Volkswagens until October 1952 was a four-speed, non-synchromesh transaxle – i.e. the gearbox and final-drive assemblies are in one combined unit. After that date export models were equipped with synchromesh on the three higher forward gears.

So as to increase ground clearance, and therefore improve driving ability over rough terrain, all Type 82 Kübelwagen models and certain wartime Beetle saloons were equipped with reduction gears on the outer ends of the rear axles. These gears stepped the drive down so that the centreline of the wheel was now below that of the driveshaft, at the same time effectively reversing the rotation of the axle. To allow for this, the crownwheel was placed on the opposite side of the differential unit (a mechanical, cam-operated, limited slip type) when compared to a 'civilian' specification

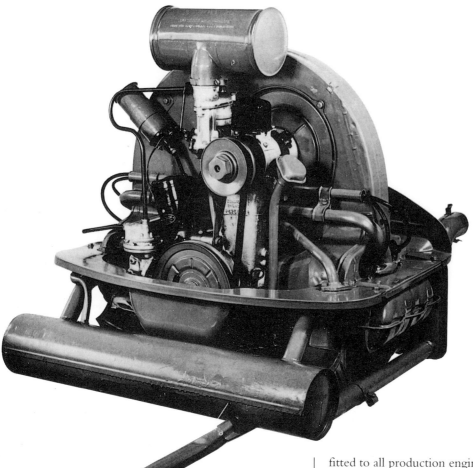

The four-cylinder, horizontally-opposed Volkswagen engine is an engineering masterpiece with a light, magnesium-alloy crankcase, forged crankshaft and an ingenious cooling system.

Beetle, so as to reverse the drive from the transmission.

The gear cluster and final drive assembly are housed in a magnesium alloy casing which is split longitudinally in a vertical plane. This means that any work on the transmission necessitates its removal from the vehicle.

The engine is a classic of engineering design. In simple terms, it is a horizontally-opposed – 'boxer' – four-cylinder, air-cooled, four-stroke engine. It comprises a magnesium alloy two-piece crankcase with separate cast-iron cylinders, aluminium pistons and forged connecting rods. A forged steel crankshaft runs in four plain bearings, while the camshaft – driven directly off the crankshaft – runs directly in the crankcase on all engines built prior to August 1965.

The very first engines fitted to Kübelwagens were only 985cc, but in 1943 the capacity was increased to 1131cc, with a power output of just 25bhp. For the 1954 model year the power output was increased to 30bhp and the capacity to 1192cc, this remaining unchanged until the end of the decade.

The engine is cooled by a large fan mounted on the end of the dynamo, this in turn being driven by a belt from the end of the crankshaft. An oil cooler is fitted to all production engines, and was located on top of the crankcase, inside the characteristic D-shaped fan housing. Pressed-steel shrouds over the cylinders and cylinder heads ensure an even flow of cool air over the engine.

The single downdraught carburettor is fed by a mechanical fuel pump driven by pushrod and cam off the distributor drive shaft, the latter being driven from the crankshaft by a skew gear. With a small carburettor, modest inlet valves, and a long inlet manifold necessitated by the boxer engine design, the engine is unable to rev very high, therefore making long-term reliability one of the Volkswagen engine's prime attributes.

Unfortunately, because so many of the special-bodied vehicles built after the war were styled as sports cars rather than family saloons, the performance offered by the standard engine did not match up to the looks. From the outset, Dr Porsche had himself realised the potential that lay in the Volkswagen engine for increasing power output, as had the likes of Major Hirst and Colonel McEvoy when the British took charge of the factory in 1945. At the very least, the addition of an extra carburettor allowed the engine to rev far more freely than would otherwise have been possible, giving greater power and a higher top speed.

Throughout the 1950s there was a variety of tuning conversions available for the Volkswagen

Wolfgang Denzel also produced a 1300cc conversion for the 30bhp Volkswagen engine. This too featured special cylinder heads, dual carburettors and a forged crankshaft. Competition versions were capable of producing in excess of 90bhp from just 1281cc.

engine, the most famous of these being that manufactured by Oettinger Kraftfahrttechnische Spezialanstalt, or Okrasa as it is better known. The Okrasa conversion for the 1131cc Volkswagen engine was available in two forms to suit the customer's pocket. The basic kit consisted of a pair of Okrasa's own-design cylinder heads, which featured separate inlet ports for each cylinder and larger valves, a pair of Solex 32PBI carburettors, matching manifolds, air-cleaners and all linkages. The cylinder heads were available with either 7.5:1 or 8.5:1 compression ratio. When installed on a healthy 30bhp engine, the basic Okrasa kit resulted in a 33% increase in power, and a corresponding increase in torque. However, the most impressive results were obtained using the full Okrasa conversion, entitled the TSV-1300/30. This increased the capacity from the basic 1192cc to nearer 1300cc – 1293cc to be precise. The increase in cubic capacity was achieved by fitting a forged crankshaft with a stroke of 69.5mm compared with the original 64mm. With the dual Solex carburettors, Okrasa's special cylinder heads and a mildly reground camshaft, the TSV-1300/30 engine produced in the region of 48bhp – a very useful increase in power. Marketed in America by European Motor Products Inc of Riverside – later to become known simply as EMPI – the Okrasa conversions were without doubt the most popular.

A similar conversion was available from Denzel in Austria, manufacturer of a sports car of its design. This also included a pair of special cylinder heads with larger valves and separate inlet ports, as well as Porsche-like rectangular exhaust ports to further help breathing. An engine capacity of 1281cc was achieved by the use of Denzel's own 67mm stroker crankshaft, 78mm pistons and aluminium cylinders with chromium bores. In addition, the complete Denzel conversion included special connecting rods, manifolds, dual Solex 32PBI carburettors and all linkages and filters. Aluminum connecting rods were available for competition use. Denzel's publicity material claimed that a Beetle fitted with the complete 1300 conversion would be capable of a maximum speed of 93mph/150kmh, reaching 26mph/42kmh in first gear, 46mph/75kmh in second and 78mph/125kmh in third. Although the regular road version gave just 48bhp, Denzel claimed that up to 85bhp was available with this 1300cc conversion. In full competition trim, over 90bhp was possible. Clearly, this was more than sufficient to give Denzel's own sports car – or any other Volkswagen-based vehicle – considerably more performance than Dr Porsche ever envisaged.

While Okrasa and Denzel were the two best known VW tuning concerns in the 1950s, there were plenty of others prepared to try their hands at coaxing

more power from the people's car. The most commonplace conversion consisted of the installation of dual carburettors, either simply doubling up on the standard fitment, or occasionally substituting a pair of larger carburettors from another vehicle altogether.

The Deitz Engineering Company in Michigan, USA, marketed a very simple kit that included a pair of inlet manifolds, all necessary linkages and one extra regular Volkswagen Solex carburettor. Deitz claimed a power increase of around 18% for this conversion.

An almost identical kit was available in Germany from Autotechnik, called the Express conversion. Once again, this consisted of an extra Solex carburettor, all linkages, manifolds and filters. Express claimed a somewhat optimistic 25% increase in power with no other modification necessary.

The well-known German tuning company of Theo Decker similarly added an extra carburettor to produce the original Comet conversion kit.

An interesting departure from normal practice was the German Fischer dual carburettor conversion. This dispensed with the Solex carburettor altogether and replaced it with a pair of Amal slide carburettors more commonly seen on motorcycles. The conversion was marketed in the USA by Competition Chemicals of Iowa and resulted in a modest increase in horsepower from 30bhp to 34bhp. Although insufficient to give greatly increased performance, the Fischer dual carburettor conversion allowed the driver to use higher engine revs when overtaking. Quite what the fragile 30bhp crankshaft had to say about that remains unrecorded.

The British were not prepared to be left out of this game, and a number of conversions were available for the Volkswagen engine from the mid-1950s. One such was the Tarrant and Frazer twin-carburettor conversion which, in common with the Express and Deitz kits, added an extra Solex carburettor to increase the maximum speed by approximately 4mph/7kmh. Similar kits were available from Adams (VW) Conversions of London – the AVC kit – and the West Essex Engineering Co. There was also the Rally Equipment conversion.

However, for the person who did not wish to completely rebuild his engine in order to fit an Okrasa or Denzel conversion, there were alternatives to these simple carburettor kits: superchargers. Today, the idea of supercharging such an apparently frail engine as the 30bhp Volkswagen might seem faintly absurd, but there were two companies in the 1950s which offered

One of the most popular modifications in the 1950s was the Okrasa conversion (left). This consisted of a pair of special cylinder heads, dual carburettors and a long-stroke crankshaft. With a capacity of 1293cc, the Okrasa conversion offered around 48bhp.

The American Judson supercharger (right) was another popular conversion of the time. It relied on the original Solex carburettor, suitably rejetted, and could be persuaded to push the Beetle to around 80mph/130kmh! Power output was around 48bhp.

blowers for VWs. The best known was the American Judson concern, which produced a rotary-vane type supercharger suitable for small-displacement engines. The Judson kit was a bolt-on conversion which took about three hours to fit to a Beetle or Karmann Ghia. The standard carburettor was retained, suitably rejetted, along with the original manifold. An interesting feature of this package was the separate oil system deemed necessary to keep the bearings of the supercharger lubricated. In an otherwise standard Beetle, maximum speed was increased to almost 81mph/130kmh with a 0-62mph/100kmh time of just under sixteen seconds – a considerable improvement over the original thirty seconds or more! Power went up to around 48bhp, approximately the same as a full TSV-1300/30 Okrasa conversion.

The second supercharger kit available for the Volkswagen was the Swiss-made MAG model. This was a Roots-type blower, driven – as was the Judson – by a V-belt from the crankshaft pulley. Manufactured by Motosacoche SA of Geneva, the MAG blower boosted to 4psi and cut the 0-60mph time to around twenty-one seconds. The MAG was in many ways a more convincing conversion, appearing better engineered and no longer reliant on the tiny standard

carburettor, instead using a Solex 32mm unit.

As far as being able to make full use of all this new-found power was concerned, there were several ways in which the owner of a VW-based special could improve the handling and braking of his vehicle. For example, simply adding the front anti-roll bar from a Karmann Ghia coupé improved matters dramatically, while lowering the rear suspension – easily achieved by adjusting the angle of the trailing arms on the splined torsion bars – could give Porsche-like handling. When it came to the braking system, Porsche conveniently sorted out any deficiencies in that department. The large aluminium-drummed brakes fitted to the 356 were a simple bolt-on conversion for any Volkswagen, although most owners tended to remain loyal to the VW's cast-iron drums.

So, what could be better? A readily available chassis that lent itself to the fitment of virtually any style of body, an unburstable engine that could be tuned to give more than double its original horsepower and a transmission that was both compact and rugged. Quite apart from any economic, historical or political considerations, it is easy to see why the Volkswagen became such a popular basis for special-bodied and coachbuilt cars.

THE EARLY YEARS
FIRST VARIATIONS ON A THEME

From the outset, Dr Porsche had envisaged his basic design being put to use in a variety of rôles, from delivery van to – unlikely though it may seem – racing car. In 1938 he built three streamlined Volkswagen-based sports cars to compete in the much-vaunted Berlin-Rome road race of 1939. Although the race never took place owing to the start of hostilities, the three vehicles survived to be used as personal transport by high-ranking officials. One of the cars was destroyed in an accident during the war, another was 'liberated' by American soldiers in 1945 and subsequently run into the ground, while the third – thought to be Porsche's own car – survived to be raced by an Austrian driver with some success in the early 1950s.

However, other early variants were far more prosaic, being born out of necessity rather than imagination. The best-known of these is the Type 82 Kübelwagen, of which some 50,000 were built during the war between 1940 and April 1945. Many variations on the Kübelwagen theme appeared during the war, including the versatile four-wheel drive Type 166 Schwimmwagen and the Type 82E – a Beetle body on the raised Kübelwagen running gear. There was even a four-wheel drive version of the Beetle produced in limited numbers designated the Type 87, along with a host of confusingly-numbered other variations. The confusion centres round the Type numbers given to each vehicle, firstly by Porsche's design team, then the military and finally by the factory after the war.

The Type 166 Schwimmwagen was a four-wheel drive amphibious vehicle. The propeller was driven off the crankshaft, and could be hinged out of the way when not in use.

Different vehicles were sometimes given apparently identical project numbers, while one vehicle might be given two conflicting designations. For historians concerned with the military VW, the mystery of Type and project numbers is a difficult one to unravel.

Amongst the vehicles that appeared immediately after the war was a series of vans, the majority of which saw service with the Reichpost (German Post office). The Type 83 was little more than a Beetle saloon with the body cut across the roof and along the waistline behind the doors. Onto this was built a simple box with a pair of hinged rear doors which overhung the rear of the vehicle. Access to the engine was achieved either via a curved lid under the rear overhang, or by way of a hatch built into the floor of the loading area. The driver and passenger of these two-seat vehicles could gain access to the rear through a small hatch built into the bulkhead. Engine cooling was evidently a problem with the Type 82 range, for later versions could be seen with a row of louvres crudely fitted in each quarter panel in addition to those seen in the rear engine lid. Presumably the ungainly box conversion upset the flow of air round the back of the van, starving the engine of air.

Before the Beetle-based Type 83, a Kübelwagen-derived van was built for the postal service, designated the Type 28, although production was shelved due to the lack of available body pressings.

In 1939 Porsche was ready to compete in the Berlin-Rome road race with three streamlined racing cars built on the Volkswagen chassis. **Because of the outbreak of war the event never took place, and the cars became used for transport by Nazi officials.**

There were other official variations, too, including a pick-up Beetle (Type 81), a fire-tender Kübelwagen (the Type 25) and a strange short-wheelbase 'road tractor' Beetle (Type 100).

Among the 'not-so-official' models was a pick-up often seen around Wolfsburg towing a tubular steel trailer designed to carry a single Beetle. This, according to Ivan Hirst, was not a factory project as had been supposed, but the work of a local garage owner – possibly Schwen – shortly after the war, and was used to carry Beetles for repair. The pick-up was evidently a professionally-built vehicle, based, it would seem, on a Type 82E, the high ground clearance suggesting a Kübelwagen chassis. At the rear, a single hinged door gave access to the engine, while cooling air was drawn in through a set of very stylish louvres punched into the quarter panels behind the rear wheels. The vehicle was seen in two forms, with and without a well-fitting steel extension to the pick-up bed which had a drop-down tailgate secured by a pair of latch pins.

Very early on in the Beetle programme, a cabriolet version had been part of the plan. Indeed, a cabriolet had even taken part in the original factory cornerstone ceremony in 1938.

When the Beetle began to rise out of the Wolfsburg ashes in 1945, the first priority was to re-establish production of the saloon model. Ivan Hirst, however, soon realised the advantages of an expanded model range for the future and gave the task of producing a cabriolet to ex-Porsche man Rudolf Ringel, who was in charge of the experimental shop. The factory-produced cabriolet was in very much the same form as that of the pre-war examples. These rare new Beetle cabriolets – only two or three were built – were designated Type 15.

The most significant differences between these early examples and the later production models built by Wilhelm Karmann at Osnabrück lay with the windscreen surround and the rear engine lid. On the KdF-derived cabriolets, the windscreen was identical to that of the regular saloon model, mounted in a surround that sloped gently down at each end. In fact, the surround was little more than the front portion of a saloon's roof pressing. As Karmann and Hebmüller were later to discover, this surround did not have sufficient strength to withstand repeated fastening and unfastening of the folding roof, with the result that the windscreen glass could be broken all too easily. To cure this problem, both Karmann and Hebmüller opted for new square-cornered windscreens and surrounds.

At the rear, the folding roof took up much of the space normally occupied by the air intake louvres below the rear window of the saloon models, so the early cabriolets featured two sets of louvres – a truncated row on the main body below the folding roof, and a second row stamped into the engine lid. Aesthetically this was not an ideal solution to the cooling problem, and when full production began at Karmann the rear of the car was redesigned so that all louvres were incorporated in the engine lid alone.

There were other differences between these early cabriolets and later models. The first examples had Kübelwagen-like semaphore indicators mounted externally on the front quarter panels just ahead of the doors, whereas later examples saw the semaphores fitted flush, also in the front quarter panels. Only the production cabriolets had the semaphores mounted in the quarter panels behind the doors.

The Type 82 Kübelwagen was the mainstay of the German armed forces. It was a simple vehicle with two-wheel drive only. The body was made by the Ambi-Budd factory in Berlin, which was part American owned.

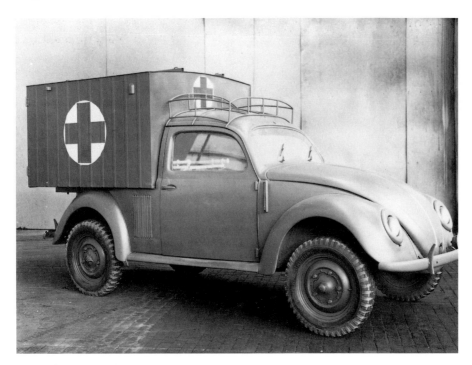

The Type 83 Beetle-derived van was put to many uses. Originally intended for use by the German postal service, it was pressed into service as an ambulance. Length was a problem – a hole needed to be cut into the bulkhead to allow for the stretcher.

In the front wings, just below and slightly inboard of the headlights, a pair of flush-mounted horns were fitted where, at a later stage, the smaller horn grills were fitted.

These early cabriolets were little more than saloons with the roof sliced off, for it took Karmann a considerable amount of effort to turn the idea into a realistic proposition for production.

Perhaps the most exciting of all early conversions was what has become known as the Radclyffe roadster. The story of this attractive two-seater begins before the Second World War with Michael McEvoy. McEvoy had been educated at Eton and was a Rolls-Royce apprentice; he was the son of portrait painter Ambrose McEvoy. When Michael inherited some family money, he proceeded to spend much of his new-found wealth building racing motorcycles under the McEvoy name. He then turned his attention from motorcycles to cars, tuning and developing mundane models like Morrises and Wolseleys to produce what he sold as 'McEvoy Specials'. With partners, he acquired the rights to the Zoller supercharger, and then worked as consultant to Mercedes-Benz, which resulted in the company's racing cars being supercharged to great effect. During this spell with Mercedes-Benz, McEvoy had the opportunity to ride in the new Volkswagen in company with a number of foreign journalists at the 1938 Berlin motor show.

By the end of the war, Colonel McEvoy, as he had then become, was a senior officer in the Royal Electrical and Mechanical Engineers (REME) and had already befriended Major Ivan Hirst. His rôle at this time was to organise the supervision of the various German repair workshops – effectively the post-war motor trade – so as to make best possible use of the available resources to keep Germany mobile. He was therefore responsible at this stage for a part of the Volkswagen factory at Wolfsburg engaged in the overhaul of ex-German army trucks, and Jeep engines for the British Army.

It was McEvoy's idea to put the Volkswagen back into production, if possible, in order to provide the occupying authorities with light vehicles at no cost to the British tax payer. According to Ivan Hirst, McEvoy was a man who was always coming up with a bright idea.

He came to Wolfsburg one day in 1946, full of enthusiasm for producing a Volkswagen-based racing car very much along the lines of the 500cc formula cars then becoming popular in Britain. He asked his friend Rudy Uhlenhaut, the man responsible for the design of Mercedes-Benz's pre-war racing cars, to sketch out some ideas – these included turning the engine and transmission round to improve weight distribution.

Hirst did not share McEvoy's enthusiasm for such a project, telling him, 'Look Michael, we have enough trouble making normal saloons without getting involved in this. If you want to think about it, you go and think about it'. However, this did set Hirst wondering whether a two-seat Volkswagen might be an interesting exercise for Ringel's experimental

One of the earliest unofficial conversions was this pick-up. The high ride height suggests that it was based on a Type 82E, with reduction gears on the rear axles. It was often seen around the factory and is believed to have been used by a local garage for collecting vehicles for service and repair.

Major Ivan Hirst at the wheel of one of the first post-war cabriolets assembled by the British. Note the curved windscreen surround.

Perhaps the most intriguing of all early conversions was the so-called Radclyffe Roadster. It was built in 1946 at Major Hirst's request by the experimental workshop. The engine cover was a modified front bonnet pressing.

The roadster was an attractive car and it almost certainly provided the inspiration for Joseph Hebmüller to build the first of his own roadsters.

workshop. He sketched out some ideas, including the use of a front bonnet at the rear to produce a two-seat roadster. This was duly built, although some panel beating disguised the origins of the sloping rear bodywork, and Hirst asked his chief at headquarters, Colonel Charles Radclyffe, if he'd like to use it during the summer months.

Hirst has no doubts that this car was the inspiration for the Hebmüller roadster that was subsequently built, as Joseph Hebmüller would almost certainly have seen the so-called Radclyffe roadster on his visits to the factory around this time.

The car was equipped with twin carburettors which, Ivan Hirst recalls, improved the performance but at the expense of flexibility – flat-spots in carburation were never fully cured. It saw regular service in Radclyffe's hands, periodically returning to the factory for servicing. On one occasion Radclyffe telephoned Hirst to say that his driver had had a bit of trouble and

could he send a recovery vehicle to collect the car. The next morning, Hirst went down to the repair shops to see what the problem was. There was not a scratch on the car, yet clearly something was very much amiss for the front wheels were tucked back in the wheel arches.

It transpired that the driver, while on his way from the factory, had skidded onto a steel girder lying by the side of the Autobahn. This had ripped out the underbelly of the car, smashed its way through the transmission, hit the flywheel and knocked the crankshaft back in the crankcase! A replacement chassis and engine were fitted and the car sent on its way once more. It is because two chassis numbers were therefore allocated to the roadster that some authorities have wrongly assumed two such vehicles existed. Unfortunately, the fate of the Radclyffe roadster is unknown.

However, predating this by some three or four

years is the remarkable – and decidedly unofficial – sports car built on a Type 82 Kübelwagen chassis. The story began in July 1943 when the German armed forces evacuated Cap Bon and a camp was set up by a British unit at La Marsa, Tunisia. At the instigation of the commanding officer of the 123rd and 849th SRI Company, US Airforce, a Captain Christian, along with some helpers, built a sports car of sorts from the remains of a burnt-out Kübelwagen and parts of a wrecked aircraft.

The vehicle, nicknamed the Thunderbolt, was a bizarre-looking creation, with a high fin tail and a windscreen clearly pirated from an aircraft cockpit. The Kübelwagen desert-specification balloon tyres looked slightly out of keeping on what was intended to be a sports car!

A friend of Captain Christian, RAF Flight Lieutenant W K H Jeffrey (seen at the wheel in the photograph) recalls that the Thunderbolt handled extremely well over the rough terrain in the area and also that Captain Christian had plans to ship the car back to the USA at the end of the war. Whether that ever happened is unknown, as is the ultimate fate of the vehicle. While the Thunderbolt may not have been the most glamorous of special-bodied Volkswagens, it was certainly one of the first built by anyone outside either the factory or the Porsche workshops. It was a taste of things to come...

Above is a fascinating car built in North Africa from the remains of a Type 82 Kübelwagen by members of the US Airforce in 1943. It featured a body made from parts of an aircraft, including the cockpit. Note the use of the original desert sand tyres.

Top is the unusual and somewhat ungainly sports car built by Kurt Kuhnke, based on Volkswagen components. It was typical of many early home-built racing cars.

PRODUCTION
THE SERIES-BUILT MODELS

By no means all coachbuilt Volkswagens were the product of an enterprising individual who simply wished to build a single car to suit his own personal taste. Many companies took it upon themselves to put one or more of their designs into production, with certain concerns, such as Karmann, gaining the full backing of Wolfsburg.

While some of the better known companies are covered in greater detail elsewhere in this book, there were others less well known for whom the challenge of producing a series of special-bodied Volkswagens was too great to resist. In some cases this was as a result of receiving a commission from a wealthy client, in others because the coachbuilders themselves identified a place in the market for a new product.

Wendler

The Wendler family business was originally formed in 1840 when Erhard Wendler, following an apprenticeship as a gunsmith, decided to venture into the lucrative coachbuilding market. At first located in cramped premises in Wilhelmstrasse, Reutlingen, the business grew until 1863 when it moved to new workshops in Lederstrasse, also in Reutlingen.

In 1871, Erhard handed the business over to his two sons, Adolf and Karl, the latter retiring in 1902. His nephew, also named Karl, joined the company in 1909. The business flourished, but concern was expressed about its long term future as traditional horse-drawn coaches were becoming a thing of the past. The motorized vehicle was seen as the way ahead.

The company received a boost when a young designer by the name of Helmut Schwandner joined the staff in the early 1920s. Schwandner was fascinated by automobiles, attending courses in technical design and occasionally receiving brochures from his brother in the United States which showed how car styling was developing across the Atlantic. Adolf Wendler was quick to appreciate Schwandner's talent for design and

he soon assumed a leading role in the company.

However, when the Second World War brought a halt to all private car production, Wendler was put under the control of the military, which placed more importance on the conversion of luxury cars into ambulances than the creation of beautifully aerodynamic limousines. It was not until 1945 that Wendler could once again turn its hand to coachbuilding.

The first Volkswagen-based vehicle to come out of the Reutlingen factory was a very pleasing station wagon, or woodie, to use the American description. The vehicle, based on a wartime KdF-Wagen, was converted by Wendler for company use and could still be seen on the streets around the workshops as late as 1963. It was unusual in that the roof panel was made of steel, unlike most other similar vehicles on which the roof is made of fabric or wood. The side panels and doors were entirely fabricated from wood, a long side window in the rear quarters being divided by a single upright.

Clearly visible in the one known photograph of Wendler's station wagon is the high ride height brought about by the retention of the original Kübelwagen-style suspension used on the military version of the KdF-Wagen. Also visible is the seam across the roof just behind the windscreen where the new roof panel was spliced into the original bodywork.

However attractive the station wagon might have been, Wendler is best known for its sports cars featuring stylish bodies in the Porsche mould. The first of these formed part of a limited series of cars produced in 1950 for an American client. The attractive roadster was essentially a two-seater, although a third person could be carried thanks to a small transverse seat located in the rear. The body was aluminium over a frame of wood and steel, with a simple lightweight fabric hood to keep out the worst of the weather. The doors were rear-hinged, suicidestyle, and featured frameless wind-up windows made, as was the curved windscreen, by Securit.

Wendler is best known for its Porsche-like sports cars, which dated back to 1950. The bodies were made of aluminium over a frame of wood and steel.

Wendler's first post-war vehicle was this Type 82E-based station wagon, with steel roof and wooden sides. It was seen as recently as 1963.

Two years later, Wendler received a commission from Fabr. Martini in Augsburg for another roadster, this example being powered by a Porsche engine. Although similar to the earlier car, the 1952 Wendler had far clumsier styling, with polished trim detracting from the otherwise simple lines.

In 1957, a commission was received from another American client to produce a small series of two-seat roadsters, the styling of which still failed to equal that of the original 1950 model. Longer and lower, the new vehicle was again built of aluminium over a wood and steel frame, with imitation leather used as the upholstery material.

Wendler, like many other coachbuilders of the time, had connections with Porsche, the association leading to Wendler producing the historic Porsche

In contrast to the sleek Wendler is the unusual Hartman. A series of ten of these saloon models was built by Karosserie Hartman in Czechoslovakia in or around 1946. The most dominant feature was the Buick-like front grille.

The rear-hinged doors opened to reveal a very heavy dashboard with the most basic instrumentation. The interior trim was simple.

550 Spyder models for sale to the general racing public in 1956. Wendler was also involved in the production of a prototype model for Porsche as late as 1960.

Hartman

In stark contrast to the generally stylish and sporting creations of Wendler, the series of ten four-seater saloons built by Karosserie Hartman in Czechoslovakia was obviously influenced by American styling of the era. Little is known today of the firm other than that these ten vehicles were produced in or around 1946, using the Type 82 Kübelwagen chassis as a base. The body was a fastback design with stylized front wings and bonnet echoing the latest models from Detroit.

At the front a grille similar in style to that of the 1950 Buick served as nothing other than embellishment, for cooling air was ducted to the rear-mounted engine by two ear-like scoops aft of the side windows. Access to the 30bhp engine currently fitted (which incidentally retains the original Kübelwagen fan-housing and heavy-duty air filter) was via a cavernous lid that resembled the trunk of a 1940 Chevrolet.

Inside the Hartman the dashboard is very heavy and box-like, with basic instrumentation and controls laid out in a casual fashion. The banjo-style steering wheel is most likely a later fitment from an early Porsche, or maybe an accessory part from Petri. Today, the car is upholstered in red cloth with neat wood trim round the inside of the windows.

The Hartman remains a fine example of the great lengths to which coachbuilders were prepared to go in order to produce a 'new' car out of whatever wartime

surplus was at hand. The market for new models was clearly there but the raw materials, sadly, were not.

Coenen

One of the more common conversions of the early post-war years was the fitting of a full-length or roll-back sunroof to conventional saloon models. One of the first companies to carry out this conversion was W F Coenen who modified a wartime KdF-Wagen for a client in 1947. Nothing more is known about the vehicle other than what can be gleaned from the sole remaining photograph.

The Tuscher roll-back roof conversion gave almost cabriolet-like motoring without the expense. However, much of the original saloon's rigidity was lost.

The only surviving Drews is this 1949 or 1950 model. Just discernible are the art deco-like grilles which allow cooling air to reach the rear-mounted engine.

Tuscher

Tuscher of Zurich, on the other hand, is known to have produced something between twenty and thirty full-length sunroof models for the Swiss government, beginning in 1949. Today three of these cars – a 1948, a 1949 and a later 1954 model – are known to survive in Switzerland, while a fourth is now in California.

The conversion was a simple one, the original roof section from a few inches behind the windscreen back to just below the rear window being sliced out and the edges made good. The cooling louvres beneath the rear window were somewhat crudely capped off with a new strip of metal. The roof itself was of canvas on a simple wood and metal frame, with a heavy wooden header bow at the front which swung back on two long struts pivoted just above the rear side windows. The header was locked into place above the wind-screen with two mortice locks operated by a pair of carriage handles.

The Tuscher was not an exotic conversion, and clearly resembled the pre-war sunroof models produced by the factory. However, the conversion was a good one and professionally executed.

Drews

In 1938 the Drews brothers, Gerhard, Erwin and Werner, formed a *Karosserie* in Berlin, moving to Wuppertal in the Ruhr shortly after the Second World

War. In common with other such companies, Drews concentrated most of its efforts on repairing damaged vehicles, but after carrying out some work preparing Ford and Mercedes cars for racing, they looked around for other sources of income.

One of the earliest jobs the company carried out was the conversion of a abandoned Type 82E (the two-wheel drive version of the wartime Type 87 Beetle) into a pick-up for their own use as a delivery vehicle, but the brothers had their sights set on more exciting projects and in 1948 they produced their first sports car. Along with Denzel, Drews became one of

The Drews was very box-like in plan, with slab-like sides broken only by some simple trim. In this photograph it is just possible to make out the flat-topped steering wheel.

From straight ahead, the clumsiness of the trim on the Drews can be fully appreciated. The heavy framing to the windscreen reduced the visibility greatly.

A Swedish customer placed an order for a slightly different version of the Dews roadster with a curved, one-piece windscreen and less ornate trim.

the first companies to go into production with a Volkswagen-based vehicle anywhere in the world.

Viewed from above, the sports car was extremely square in shape, with a distinctly art deco feel to it. The chassis was, almost inevitably, that of a Volkswagen Beetle, but the Drews' origins are hard to identify at first sight thanks to the lengthy overhangs at front and rear.

The frontal treatment was again in the Porsche vein, with swept-back wings, Beetle headlights and a long, curved bonnet leading back to a butted two-piece windscreen. The front and rear bumpers were specially made.

Although the car was designed as a 2+2, interior space was somewhat limited, the rear seats being too small for anyone other than a child. Likewise, the luggage space in the front was little different to that of a Beetle despite the much larger overall dimensions of the car. However, the level of interior trim was good, with the dashboard housing the familiar Beetle glove boxes and instrument panel. Seats were usually from a Beetle but more luxurious ones could be supplied to order.

In the original version, the steering wheel was a specially-made item, flat at the top to aid vision over the top of the dashboard. The driver needed all the help he could get as far as visibility was concerned, for the central dividing bar of the windscreen was very heavy in section. On at least one later model, only a single windscreen wiper was fitted, fortunately to the driver's side!

The aluminium bodies were hand-formed over a

steel frame, with wide doors – rear-hinged on early models – giving easy access to the interior. Aluminium trim was used both internally and externally. In some instances the trim was extremely heavy in section, giving the car a most distinctive and almost toy-like appearance.

The greatest problem faced by Drews, in common with many others, was how to obtain the chassis necessary to build the cars. The Wolfsburg factory had always been reluctant to supply bare chassis to coachbuilders, perhaps fearing that the more exciting models which might result would tempt potential customers away from the Beetle, so Drews was forced to buy complete cars, either new or used, and strip off the Beetle body. Sometimes a bare chassis could be purchased from a helpful Volkswagen dealership, but such opportunities were undoubtedly rare.

The Drews sports car was truly a hand-built vehicle, with up to 1000 man hours spent on each one. Labour costs being relatively high, the price of a coachbuilt car like the Drews was beyond the pocket of all but a fortunate few. Initially demand was slow, batches of ten or so cars at a time leaving the coach-works, but with demand slowly increasing the time to build each car was gradually reduced, resulting in a slight drop in price. Even so, by the end of production in 1951 only 150 had been produced.

In addition to the production model some special-order versions were produced. One of these, for a Swedish customer, featured more rounded frontal styling without most of the heavy aluminium trim common to most Drews. However, as if to compen-

The vehicles of Wolfgang Denzel saw use in competition from the start. This prototype was driven with success in the 1949 Austrian Alpine Rally.

sate, the rear wings carried three extra pieces of trim just ahead of the wheel arches.

The only other known variation was a coupé model for a customer who demanded more power – this was provided by the fitting of a Porsche engine and instrumentation. In common with the Swedish roadster, the coupé did away with the normal two-piece windscreen, being fitted with a single curved glass in an aluminium frame. It even featured a wiper on the rear screen which may possibly have been the first time a car was so equipped.

Today, the Drews company is still in existence, but sadly no longer involved in the manufacture of specialist sports cars. Only one example, a 1950 version, is thought to remain.

Denzel

Across the border in Austria there were two people for whom the concept of a Volkswagen-based sports car had great appeal. One of these, Ferdinand Porsche, went on to become a household name while the other, Wolfgang Denzel, is largely known solely amongst the Volkswagen cognoscenti.

Denzel was an engineer and garage proprietor

before the war, coming from a family which for 400 years had been engaged in the craft of bell-founding. He also had a strong interest in competition, winning a Coupe Des Alpes in the 1939 French Alpine Rally behind the wheel of a BMW 328, in addition to many other successes with BMW motorcycles and cars.

In 1948, with his friend Hubert Stroinigg, Denzel designed and built a sports car based on a Type 82 Kübelwagen chassis. What the roadster lacked in power (it retained its 25bhp 1131cc engine) it more than made up for in performance owing to a low weight. At 600kg/1320lb, the first Denzel was some 120kg/265lb lighter than the contemporary Beetle.

Competition was foremost in Denzel's mind from the outset, the car being entered in the 1949 Austrian Alpine Rally – the result: first place! This and many other competition successes guaranteed a steady demand for the Austrian sports car.

The first Denzel featured a body fabricated from wood not so much through choice as through shortage of other suitable materials at the time. Although the end result was pleasing in terms of both performance and aesthetics, the wooden construction made series production uneconomic.

From the rear, the 1951 Denzel was particularly attractive. Somewhat incongruously, semaphore indicators were retained, mounted ahead of the doors.

By 1953 a production model was released with larger Lockheed-style brakes. These allowed Denzel to fit wheels of a different design, hiding the VW origins.

To satisfy demand for a low-cost but competitive sports car, Denzel took stock of the raw materials situation and embarked upon a new design. This saw the light of day in 1951 and featured a tubular steel frame designed to accept Volkswagen suspension components and an aluminium body. With a shorter wheelbase – just 2.09m/82in as opposed to 2.40m/94in – the new Denzel proved extremely manoeuvrable and, thanks in part to a Denzel-prepared 1284cc Volkswagen engine, extremely successful. Interestingly enough, the Karosseriefabrik Ferdinand Keibl Gesellschaft in Vienna, who made the bodies for Denzel, was also responsible for many of the early, 1949-51, Porsche 356 Gmünd models.

In 1953 the production version saw the light of day, with a choice of engines – a 1281cc 52bhp unit for the road, or a 1290cc 64bhp option for competi-tion. The lower power version was called the Seriensuper, while the high performance model became the Super International. The body style remained much the same as before, with the principal changes made solely to improve the product, among them the addition of large Lockheed-style brake drums that allowed the use of wheels other than those of VW origin.

Despite having the appearance of being a relatively impractical racing car, the Denzel did in fact have useful luggage space behind the front seats. These seats took the form of an individual bucket type for the driver, with a wide two-person seat for the passenger(s). Of note, considering its competition roots, were the Denzel's powerful heater, wind-up windows and efficient windscreen wipers, all of which conspired to make the Denzel an ideal clubman's racing car.

Easily mistaken for a
Hebmüller, this roadster
was built by Werner
Maier at Laufenburg in
Switzerland in 1952.
However, the short rear
lid and semaphore indi-
cators behind the doors
give the game away.
Note the Dannenhauer
& Stauss in the back-
ground.

In 1956, the sole
surviving Maier was
nick-named 'the Frog'
thanks to its green
paintwork and
matching roof, and
competed in an ice
slalom race.

It was one of the Super International models that
surprised everybody in the 1954 Alpine Rally when,
out of 87 starters and 37 finishers, Wolfgang Denzel
and co-driver Hubert Stroinigg took first place ahead
of some impressive opposition. Indeed, the legendary
Stirling Moss could only finish in tenth place at the
wheel of his Sunbeam Alpine.

The Denzel continued in much the same form
until its demise in 1959, by which time some 350 cars
had been produced. Today, the Denzel showroom in
Vienna is home to two examples of this fine Austrian
sports car, a 1954 model and a 1959 1300SS in rally
specification. How many examples exist altogether is
unknown.

Maier

It is not at all uncommon for the search for one type
of special to lead to the discovery of something
completely different. Such was the case when what
was believed to be a Hebmüller Type 14A became
available for purchase in 1979.

With a 1952 chassis (number 1-0 340 069), the
evidently professionally-built roadster, although closely
resembling a Hebmüller, was clearly not what it
seemed. The owner, the lady manager of Senn
Automobile AG in Chur, Switzerland, had instigated a
restoration that proved to be neither sympathetic nor,
as it proved, accurate. Andy Luzzi, long-standing
Volkswagen expert in Switzerland, took on the task of
overseeing the vehicle's restoration with little idea of
what stood before him.

During the winter of 1988/89, Luzzi made a major
effort to discover some of the car's history, eventually
tracking down the first three owners via the records of
the Swiss Federal Department of Motor Vehicles.
Much to Luzzi's delight, the original owner, Herr
Geissberger, had retained all the paperwork relating to
the roadster. And so the story began to unfold...

The conversion proved to be the brainchild of
Werner Maier of Laufenburg, whose coachworks
specialised in converting saloon cars into cabriolets.
Although Morrises and Lancias were the normal fare,
any car could be converted to order and an approach
from J E Rock Volkswagen dealership in Basel led to
the construction of three of the Hebmüller-like roadsters in 1952.

The partially dismantled Beetles were towed sixty
kilometres to the Karosserie Karl Rusterholz at

Wadenswil, near Zurich, where the actual coachwork was carried out. Work on the Beetles was swiftly performed, with each conversion completed in under six weeks. However, at 9800 Swiss Francs, the list price for the finished product was almost double that of a conventional deluxe Beetle saloon, and half as much again as a Karmann cabriolet (6500 Swiss Francs), ensuring that demand was low. Even the Maier family themselves were unable to justify using one of their own roadsters due to the high cost.

The sole surviving example was driven for almost 88,000km by the original owner during a period of five years. He kept a meticulous record of every purchase and service relating to the car, and also recalled having competed in an ice slalom race in Basel in 1956. During his ownership the car was painted green with a matching folding roof, earning the nickname 'the Frog'.

The second owner, Herr Werren, a German welder, purchased the car for 3000 Swiss Francs in 1958. He began to repair and modernise the car, adding such things as later bumpers, engine, lights, etc. He discovered that the design of the folding roof made the car ideal for smuggling as, when the roof was folded away, a 'secret' compartment, out of the reach of customs officers, was to be found between the seats and the engine bay!

In 1967 the Maier roadster was sold to a Fraülein Rutener who, quite coincidentally, later became the secretary of Herr Geissberger, the original owner. The car then disappeared until 1979 when it was rediscovered in St Margrethen, on the edge of Lake Konstanz.

To get into an Enzmann, you use the step moulded into the side and climb into the cockpit. There are many noteworthy features including the use of Type 2 front indicators, heavy side trim and the air scoop in the rear lid.

The missing years cannot as yet be accounted for, although the car was rumoured to have made its way to San Francisco, California, at some point.

The Maier remains one of the prettiest conversions carried out in those early post-war years and a fine example of the skills that were available at the time. It is a pity that the high cost of the finished item did not encourage greater demand.

Enzmann

Of all the special-bodied cars built during the 1950s, the Enzmann remains without doubt one of the most futuristic. Even today, with suitable wheels and running gear, the flamboyant roadster would hardly look out of place in the car park of the local bistro. Yet this streamlined, Porsche Spyder-like sports car was first conceived in 1953, finally reaching production just three years later.

The idea for producing such an impressive vehicle came from Dr Emil Enzmann, eldest of five sons of the proprietor of the Adler Garage in Schupfheim, close to Lucerne in Switzerland. Initially, a prototype body was constructed from steel over a wooden frame and mounted on the ubiquitous Volkswagen chassis. After a little restyling here and there, the body was prepared and a mould taken from it, for the Enzmann

47

Because of their glass-fibre construction, Enzmanns have survived better than many other special-bodied Volkswagens. This example was seen at a recent Volkswagen show.

was unusual in that it was made of glassfibre at a time when aluminium was more normal.

The advantages of glassfibre as a material were legion, as it was inexpensive, simple to use and resulted in a much lighter bodyshell. The first Enzmann body was moulded by the Neuenburg concern of Schoelly, while later examples were produced by Stampfli in Granson-am-Neuenberger-See. Once moulded, the finished bodies were shipped back to the Adler Garage where the Enzmanns completed the build.

The hand-laid bodies were very simple to produce, with just three principal mouldings: the main body structure and the front and rear lids. No doors were fitted to the car as Dr Enzmann felt that their inclusion would weaken the structure too much. However, as a nod towards some sort of practicality, stepping points, resembling air scoops, were moulded into the sides of the body to facilitate entry and exit.

Inside the Enzmann, two specially-made bucket seats were fitted, in front of which lay a padded dash-board with simple instrumentation consisting of a speedometer and switches for the lighting. Owners were evidently expected to add extra gauges as they chose, for adequate room was left alongside the speedometer for a tachometer and other instruments.

Initially the Enzmann 506 (the number had no meaningful significance, being adopted following display of the car at the International Motor Show on stand number 506) was available only as an open sports car, a simple plexiglass windscreen being all the protection afforded to the occupants. However, at a later date – and presumably as a result of pressure from potential customers – a glass windscreen from a Karmann Ghia was added, along with an optional hinged hardtop. Unfortunately, these additions did little to improve the simple lines of the car.

Mechanically, the Enzmann 506 relied on the tried and trusted Volkswagen running gear and could be purchased with a choice of engines according to taste and pocket. With an all-up weight of just 550kg/1210lb, even with a basic 30bhp engine the Enzmann was not too sluggish. However, most customers opted for a more powerful Denzel or Okrasa unit, or asked for a supercharger from Judson or MAG to be fitted to the standard VW engine.

In pursuit of real performance the Enzmann brothers equipped one of their own vehicles with a Porsche Carrera motor, which must have resulted in truly exhilarating performance. Another was equipped with a roller-bearing 1500S Porsche unit tuned to give around 95bhp.

Almost unbelievably, the Enzmann 506 was available until 1968, which is an incredible testimony to the advanced styling. Other than the products of Karmann, how many specialist body designs can boast having been available over such a long period of time?

Rear view of the Australian-built Proctor, with a unique sculptured surround to the Peugeot 203C rear windscreen.

The Proctor used reskinned Beetle doors. The rear side windows are also from a Beetle. Note air scoops in the rear quarter panels.

Proctor

The latest glassfibre technology was also put to good use by Ted Proctor of Sydney, Australia, when he built four sports coupés based on the Volkswagen chassis. The first of these was completed in 1958 using a 1955 chassis for Dr Vince Adcock of Newcastle, and subsequently used by him for his daily rounds as well as weekend competition.

The Proctor could never be described as a beautiful car, but contemporary road tests did comment on the fact that it attracted much critical attention wherever it was taken. The front end of the car had a certain Denzel-like quality, but from there back the Proctor was in a league of its own. The doors were simply reskinned Beetle panels, while the rear side windows were also of Beetle origin. The windscreen came from a Goliath, and the rear screen from a Peugeot 203C. The rear lights on the sole surviving example are presently from an early Type 3, which replace the original small units of unknown parentage. Headlights are the common-or-garden Beetle sloping units, while door handles and horn grilles are from the same source.

In its original form, the Proctor featured a dashboard not dissimilar to the basic Beetle design, with a glove box and basic instrumentation, but extra gauges could be supplied. The seats were individual bucket type and were made without springs, relying on glassfibre shells to which Dunlopillo pads and imitation leopardskin covers had been added. Interestingly, the original metal seat frames were retained, resulting in

the seat backs extending up to neck level – for greater comfort, it was said. Quite what the result of a substantial rear-end shunt would have been in terms of the occupant's spine is open to debate.

The seating position was, of necessity, low and required a degree of contortion when entering or exiting. Mechanical noise was high – a combination of early transmission, air-cooling and a glassfibre body made driving for long spells tiring. However, few other sports cars were any better in this respect.

The Proctor handled and performed well, the modest overall weight no doubt being a major contributor to its good nature. A road test in the

The Ascort was also built in Australia with a glassfibre body, and designed by Mirek Craney, a Czechoslovakian emigré. Graham Lees has his work cut out restoring this example.

Australian magazine *Wheels* reported excellent road manners, excellent fuel consumption and a high average speed capability over a lengthy test route. Mention was also made of the fact that the test car – the original prototype – was still equipped with a somewhat elderly engine. Had the very latest Denzel or Okrasa technology been taken advantage of, presumably the conclusions would have been even more favourable.

Of the four Proctors that are thought to have been built, Number 1 was eventually sold to someone who decided to butcher it to fit a Leyland V8 engine. It was subsequently written off while off-road racing. Number 2, currently owned by Barry Noble in Australia. is the sole survivor and sees regular competition use in historic events. Number 3 was also written off while racing, having been fitted with a Porsche 1300cc engine. The history and whereabouts of the possible fourth car remain a mystery.

Following the initial acclaim Proctor received many orders for his car, including, it is said, one for fifty from a dealer, but he was neither interested in nor had the capital to begin volume production, so after just four cars the Proctor story came to a close.

Ascort

'Looking like a Porsche, Karmann Ghia and some Italian iron thrown in, the Ascort TSV-1300 GT is a beautiful, plush package of plastic magic, born in the Down Under Continent.' So began the January 1960 *Foreign Car Guide's* review of the stylish Australian-built Ascort. This glassfibre-bodied sports coupé was

indeed something of a styling mixture – today the frontal treatment is very reminiscent of an Alpine 110 from France, while the rear three-quarter view is certainly very Karmann Ghia-like.

The man responsible for this attractive little car was Mirek Craney, a Czechoslovakian emigré who arrived in Australia in 1950, reportedly with just a Leica camera, a portable typewriter and a pocketful of change to his name. By 1955 he had founded his own business importing plastics machinery, slide rules and Volkswagen engine conversions. He had long dreamed of building a car to his own design, feeling disappointed with many of the so-called high-class cars of the day. He felt that he could do better as he had no need to be restrained by the shackles of practicality and mass production, both of which conspired to make virtually every car on the road a compromise of some sort or another.

In 1958 he built a quarter-scale model of his dream car, followed by a full-scale mock-up on a Volkswagen chassis. As quickly as the scheme progressed, the money began to run out. To raise capital, he formed a small private company – Continental Coachwork Pty Ltd – and sold shares to friends at home and abroad. A few changes were made to the basic design, largely to keep costs down. For example, the body styling was altered slightly to accommodate a Peugeot windscreen and Austin Westminster rear glass, while Aston Martin proved to be a source of suitable front and rear light units.

The plaster mock-up was finally completed following nine months of work with the assistance of

Harold English, and a five-piece mould was taken from it. In addition, moulds were made for the separate front and rear lids and both doors, including inside and outside skins. The first body shell was mounted onto a chassis and work began on establishing the shape and position of the seating and layout of the controls in order to produce an ergonomically sound design.

Unlike many such vehicles of its time, the Ascort had been designed from the outset with safety in mind. A tubular roll-bar was moulded into the windscreen surround to provide protection in the event of a roll-over accident, while at the rear another tubular structure was moulded into the bumper to add strength in the event of a rear-end collision.

By far the most difficult part of the project was the doors. In Mirek Craney's own words, 'Not having been burdened by previous experience, I knew what I wanted, but did not quite know how to do it'. After much thought and experimentation, Craney eventually solved the problems that had thwarted the likes of Jensen and incorporated glassfibre doors with large wind-up windows into his design. Even after 198,000 miles the doors of his original car still click shut in a reassuring manner.

Mechanically, the Ascort favoured the Okrasa TSV-1300 engine, which with its special cylinder heads, crankshaft and carburettors was capable of giving Porsche-like performance to a humble Volkswagen, and even more to a lightweight vehicle such as the Ascort. When these tuned engines were fitted, a pair of air intakes was incorporated into the rear lid to improve cooling.

The Ascort was a true four-seater, with a pair of individual bucket seats at the front and a single bench in the rear. The interior was well fitted, with full instrumentation, radio, sports steering wheel and even seat belts for the front seat occupants. A fresh-air ventilation system was incorporated, with a fan to blow cool air into the interior. By the standards of the day the Volkswagen-based Ascort was a remarkably well-equipped car and, by all accounts, built to a very high standard.

Contemporary road test reports made much of the car's good handling and excellent performance, the former aided by the use of a Karmann Ghia anti-roll bar and Porsche wheels, the latter by the meaty Okrasa engine. A top speed of no less than 96mph was recorded by *Modern Motor* magazine in May 1959, due in no small way to the obviously aerodynamically-efficient styling.

But why, if this car was so good, did production cease after just nineteen examples had been built? The

The Zelensis was another glassfibre-bodied special which bolted straight onto a Volkswagen chassis.

This early advertisement shows off the simple lines and wrap-around windscreen.

answer lies in the word compromise. Mirek Craney, as we have already discovered, did not like compromise, holding it responsible for the shortcomings of most production vehicles. He realized that to put the Ascort into full production would entail many hundreds of manhours spent finishing each car to an acceptably high standard, road testing, and tuning it to perfection ready for delivery to the customer. Such work would add considerably to the cost of each individual car, making production a far less profitable proposition. Common business sense persuaded Mirek Craney to pull the plug on the Ascort project while he was still ahead.

Today, just seven examples are believed to exist, all right-hand drive as dictated by the Australian market. As an example of 'what might have been', few can better the Ascort.

Zelensis

At the tender age of seventeen Belgian-born Raoul Thiébaut had a dream, like Mirek Craney, about building his own car. He even went so far as to mock up a cabriolet design. Two years later, he embarked on a five-year spell aboard a cargo ship, travelling the world and designing cars as he went.

On his return to Belgium, he learned the skills

associated with the manufacture of cars. Then, through contacts made while travelling the world, he gained employment in California with Industrial Plastics Service of Oakland. IPS was responsible for producing the bodywork of, amongst others, a record-breaking car called the Bardahl Streamliner.

Returning to his native land once more, Thiébaut built his first real car, based on the chassis of a split-window Beetle and called the Zelensis Type 1. *Zelensis* is a Latin word meaning 'coming from Zele', the name of a Belgian community.

The design was heavily influenced by the likes of Aston Martin, Ferrari and Maserati, and was sufficiently impressive for it to be displayed at various trade fairs across Europe. Seemingly, its plastic construction did not win the support of car body repairers, who disapproved of widespread use of non-corroding materials!

Sadly, again like Mirek Craney, Raoul Thiébaut realised that to put the Zelensis into production would require a vast capital investment. All his money had gone into building one prototype, and had he even been able to afford to begin production on a worthwhile scale, seeking homologation for the Belgian market would have swallowed the profits.

Eventually, the prototype was sold to a friend who converted it for rally use. However, a mould was

taken from the body and Thiébaut was able to begin modest production as a result. Approximately fifty cars were produced to special order between 1958 and 1962, and it is believed that around ten examples still exist. It is possible that there may be more as some Zelensis cars are thought to have been sold outside Belgium.

Today, Raoul Thiébaut owns the original car once again and it is currently being restored. The body moulds still exist and at the time of writing had been offered for sale.

Jinggansham

An altogether different creation and, it has to be said, in many ways an extremely unlikely one, is the Jinggansham. Built in 1958 by the Motor Vehicle Factory at Beijing (formerly Peking) in Communist China, the rather FIAT-like saloon car was named after the Jinggang mountains where Mao Zedong (Chairman Mao Tse-Tung) built his first revolutionary base in 1927.

Few details are available save that the little saloon was apparently built in only limited numbers using the Volkswagen chassis and running gear as a base. Early models were equipped with two doors, later ones with four. It is not known how many of the Jinggansham Volkswagens exist, but it is believed that several hundred were built.

The Jinggansham was built in China by the Motor Vehicle factory in Beijing. Dating back to 1958, the FIAT-like saloon was built in both two and four-door form.

ONE-OFFS
HOME-BUILTS, COMMISSIONS AND PROTOTYPES

As we have seen, the Volkswagen chassis was adopted by quite a number of coachbuilding concerns very early in its post-war life. What is often not appreciated is that, even before hostilities in Europe had come to an end, there were some people for whom the challenge of creating a stylish, or maybe sporting, body was too great to resist. The only problem was that there were few, if any, suitable chassis available.

All that changed, however, when the retreating German forces left behind them large numbers of stranded, damaged or otherwise immobilized Kübelwagens and KdF Beetles. The wartime exploits of these simple yet effective vehicles were legendary and many people soon realized the potential that lay beneath the familiar exterior. Just as the factory had done many years previously while developing military variants, the would-be car builders of the day took to discarding the austere military bodies to expose a chassis that could have been designed with the amateur coachbuilder in mind.

No-one can say with any degree of certainty who was the first person to attempt to create a silk purse out of the Volkswagen sow's ear, but there can have been few who preceded the exploits of J Kubinsky. Although there are no known photographs surviving of this Czechoslovakian roadster – only a crude and much-copied rendition remains – it is known that construction took place in 1947 in Czechoslovakia using an abandoned 1944 Type 82 Kübelwagen chassis.

This unknown Czechoslovakian-built roadster shares much with the Kubinsky on the next page and it is hard to deny that the styling of the two cars is very similar.

The Kubinsky roadster was built on the chassis of a 1944 Type 82 Kübelwagen and powered by a super-charged engine. Power output was raised from 25bhp to 47bhp.

Possibly one of the most outlandish creations is this Kübelwagen-based sports car found in Czechoslovakia. It was built in the late 1950s using a Type 82 chassis, but the rest of the mechanical components are of later origin.

As the Kübelwagen was equipped with reduction boxes on the rear axles in order to gain extra ground clearance, one of the first modifications that needed to be carried out was to remove the transmission from the chassis, discard the reduction gears and then refit the crown wheel on the opposite side of the pinion. Had this not been done, the roadster would have had the unusual, if somewhat useless, feature of one forward and four reverse gears! At the front, the substitution of civilian (non-offset) spindles ensured a level ride height.

The original 1131cc Kübelwagen engine was retained but, in order to bestow the car with some-what more sporting characteristics, a Roots-type supercharger was fitted. Mounted atop the original inlet manifold and drawing breath through the original downdraught carburettor, the supercharger was claimed to have offered an increase in horsepower from a modest 25bhp to a more impressive 47bhp – an increase of some 88%. However, the supercharger was fitted in such a way that it was not in continuous use, presumably much to the relief of the wartime flat-four engine. Fuel economy was a reasonable 24mpg at a constant 60mph.

The body itself was constructed of light aluminium alloy and the Kubinsky roadster is believed to have weighed a modest 10.75cwt (a little over 540kg). The styling was undoubtedly ahead of its time and suggests

Beneath the Peugeot body of this saloon car lies a Type 82 Kübelwagen chassis and running gear. The retention of the original reduction gears and offset spindles has resulted in a high ride height that looks strangely out of place on a saloon.

that the designer was a person for whom aircraft design held a fascination. The two-seater body featured two enclosed headlights mounted either side of a somewhat American-inspired grille. A simple, two-piece butted windscreen offered the occupants the merest of protection from the airstream.

With its enclosed rear wheels, the Kubinsky roadster was reminiscent of the Jaguar XK series of sports cars built in England a few years later, but with a maximum speed of around 76mph/122kmh (unsupercharged) or 87mph/140kmh (supercharged) there was little chance of the Kübelwagen-based machine keeping up with the Jaguar. Sadly, like so many other such vehicles, the Kubinsky roadster has long since disappeared without trace.

Also reputed to have been built in Czechoslovakia in 1947 is yet another open sports car that is not at all unlike the Kubinsky car – indeed it raises the question whether the two were related.

This second car has a wooden frame over which a hand-formed metal body has been built. The styling is very reminiscent of the Kubinsky roadster in as much as it features long, flowing wings with a small two-seat cockpit, tiny two-piece windscreen and a dummy grille at the front. This simply comprises aluminium strips screwed directly onto the bodywork.

Behind the cockpit, in the long tail ahead of the engine, is a third 'dickey' or rumble seat for an extra passenger. However, the occupant of this seat is offered no protection by the folding roof, which only covers the two front seats!

The vehicle survives today and sees use in its home country in classic rallies. Unfortunately little more is known at this stage, but hopefully someone will be able to shed more light on this intriguing project.

Over the years, Czechoslovakia has proved to be a rich source of special-bodied Volkswagens. Many have disappeared but a survivor, albeit in extremely poor condition, is another Kübelwagen-based sportscar unearthed in that country. There is no known history relating to this vehicle, but from what he has seen of its construction the present owner is convinced that the ungainly two-seat roadster was originally built for competition use.

To support this theory is the fact that the original disc wheels have been extensively lightened by the simple expedient of drilling them with over twenty holes each. However, in contrast, it is hard to understand why someone who sought to build a car for racing would have added such an ugly and unaerodynamic windscreen.

There are strange but noteworthy features about this roadster, for example the provision in the rear apron for a starting handle (betraying its Kübelwagen origins), and the dual exhaust tips that exit through the bodywork. Details such as the heavy swage line along the sides and on the front 'bonnet' suggest some quite sophisticated tooling or the assistance of an experienced panel beater.

Although many one-offs originated in Czechoslovakia, where abandoned Kübelwagens were plentiful after the war, the Czechs did not have a monopoly on creating unusual vehicles from wartime scrap. It is not uncommon to discover that, instead of building a new

Yet another Kübelwagen-based vehicle was this sports car built by Bunny V Ronéo of Allentown, Pennsylvania. It appeared in two forms, with and without doors, and was reputedly built using parts from an aircraft and other body panels of unknown origin.

This roadster has a body built largely of wood and is based on a 1946 Beetle. It still retains its 16-inch wheels, cable brakes and 25bhp engine.

body from scratch, some enthusiasts would seek to change the shape of a vehicle by the apparently simple expedient of transplanting the shell of an entirely different car onto its chassis. Such was the method used by persons unknown to create a Peugeot-wagen, or whatever it might have been called, in Spain.

Starting with Kübelwagen chassis number 003 344 (engine number 003 527), the military body was stripped away to leave the basic platform complete with engine and suspension, and in its place was fitted the suitably modified bodyshell of a 1938 Peugeot 202 sedan. At the rear of the car, the engine cover from a pre-1953 Beetle was fitted, albeit somewhat crudely, along with a row of louvres below the rear window to allow the engine to breathe.

Still resting on its original reduction gear and offset spindle suspension, the strange hybrid has the appearance of standing on tip-toe. Also originating from the

Type 82 Kübelwagen are the KdF logo engine ancillaries, torsion bar covers, steering wheel and gearshift knob. Indeed, for the restorer of an incomplete Type 82, this one-off would have proved a very useful source of hard-to-find parts!

In the June 1947 edition of the French magazine *Mécanique Populaire*, a story appeared concerning the sports car built by Mr Bunny V Roneo of Allentown, Pennsylvania, USA. It would appear that Mr Roneo was not impressed with the domestic offerings of the time and succeeded in acquiring two Volkswagen engines and three transmissions amongst scrap imported from Africa. This would suggest that the origins of his unique two-seater were to be found among the remains of the many Kübelwagens abandoned in the North African desert by the retreating German army.

Few mechanical details are recorded of this project

other than that it featured independent suspension and hydraulic brakes (a conversion must have been carried out to upgrade the mechanical system used on the Type 82), no transmission shaft (as one would expect with a Volkswagen type transmission) and a differential lock or limited slip differential system (presumably from the Type 82) in the four-speed manual transaxle.

As far as the body is concerned, we can see that it appeared in two forms, with and without doors. We can only guess which was the original design, but it would seem most likely that the version without doors preceded the other. Many specials have been built over the years in this form, only for the driver to later curse the inconvenience of having to climb into the vehicle.

The story goes that Bunny V Roneo built the body out of parts that included four wings from American cars, although it is hard to identify which vehicles could have been the likely donors. Although the body could hardly be described as beautiful, it was evidently functional, and sufficiently aerodynamic for the roadster to return consumption figures of around 35mpg at a steady 50mph.

Sadly there is no trace of this car today.

However, another equally strange one-off does survive, albeit in unrestored form. Tom Tolson today owns one of the cutest special-bodied Volkswagens, and its story is a fascinating one. When Tom acquired this two-seat roadster (with rumble seat) in the 1980s, having first learned of its existence some years earlier, he knew little of its history.

A trip to the Volkswagen factory archives in Wolfsburg showed that the car had started life as a regular split-window Beetle, manufactured on May 20th 1946 and delivered eight days later to the First Infantry Division, then stationed in Germany. On Tom's return to the USA, further painstaking research revealed much of the story – except for one vital piece of information: who built the car originally.

Checking back through Department of Motor Vehicles records, a Jack W Cannon was found to have owned the car when it first arrived in the USA. A search through telephone directories came up with a number in the right area and suddenly Tom found himself in contact with the first registered US owner. The story unfolded thus: Jack Cannon served in the American forces in Germany and in 1956 saw the roadster for sale at a used car lot in Frankfurt. Following its purchase, the car saw regular use in Germany during 1956, 1957 and the early part of 1958. It was then driven to the docks and shipped home to New York City on board a US Army vessel to wait the arrival of its owner.

Jack Cannon collected the car some while later and then drove home to Fort Worth, Texas, putting some miles on the recently rebuilt 25bhp motor, new shock absorbers and Firestone tyres that he had fitted prior to its trip to the USA. Three days later, the roadster found itself in its new home.

Later that year, the car was sold to a German mechanic by the name of Henry Janzen who sold it the following year to a Mrs John W Therrell. The car stayed in the Therrell family until 1979 when the current owner purchased it.

Piecing together information that exists, it would seem that the car was probably damaged by a member

The Waibel has created a lot of confusion over the years with more than one person claiming that it is a Porsche-based sports car or even a prototype. Note the Morris grille fitted as part of the unique cooling system.

57

Mystery surrounds the origins of this car. The chassis carries the number 1 - 0 143 532 and dates back to January 1950. The engine came from a 1943 Kübelwagen!

'Ugly' or 'The Pearl' – whichever way you look at it, it is certainly an interesting vehicle. The long tail includes space for storing luggage.

of the First Infantry Division in 1949. As the Army is not renowned for repairing vehicles, preferring instead to replace them, it is quite possible that the Volkswagen was sold to a serving GI. More than likely he contracted a small local coachbuilder to fabricate a roadster body, the rumble seat perhaps being a sign that he had children.

Army records show that the First Infantry Division left Germany in December 1955, so the car was probably sold to the used car lot that Jack Cannon visited in 1956 as the GI prepared to return home.

Today, the car is in need of extensive restoration, although its basically wooden construction has stood the test of time extremely well. Perhaps one day Tom Tolson will be able to fill in the few missing links in this fascinating car's history.

While the Tolson roadster, pretty though it is, can

hardly be described as exotic, occasionally a Volkswagen-based vehicle will surface that has everybody guessing at its roots. The Waibel is just such a machine.

The guessing game began when the Porsche-like sports car resurfaced in 1988 following twenty years in storage. The new owner began to trace the car's lineage and almost immediately the feeling was that this might be a 'missing' early Porsche prototype built by Hans Waibel for the Gmünd factory in the late 1940s. Further research was to prove otherwise.

Hans Waibel owned the first Volkswagen dealership in Zurich and it is true that he did have connections with the Porsche factory in those early days, having been involved with Ruprecht von Senger in the preparation of two 356 coupés for the 1948 Vienna Industrial Trade Fair. Von Senger was a Swiss businessman who organized the supply of raw materials to the Gmünd Porsche works as well as helping with the sales of the first 356s through Zurich.

Subsequently, Waibel was approached by Porsche and asked if his company would be interested in producing the first Porsche cabriolets in 1948/49. However, due to a heavy workload, Waibel reluctantly declined the offer, opening the way for Beutler to begin a long association with Porsche.

In 1948, Hans Waibel had already designed and contemplated the construction of a two-seat cabriolet based on the Volkswagen chassis. With the assistance of an engineer friend, a Herr Ausweiler, and his bodyshop apprentice, Carlo Brandle, Waibel built the

The 'Black Forest' Special is intriguing in as much as it was never completed. Work began with the purchase of a new chassis in 1947.

pretty two-seater during 1949/50, using the chassis of a badly damaged 1948 VW Beetle.

The Waibel cabriolet used the complete chassis and running gear of the Volkswagen – engine number 1-0 115 914 and chassis number 1-0 85 552 – but with one significant modification. Down the central backbone of the chassis, a 150mm diameter steel tube was inserted, the purpose of which was to duct cooling air to the engine from a grille at the front of the car.

Why the need for such additional cooling? Due to the low lines of the rear bodywork, there was insufficient space in the engine bay for the fitting of a regular Volkswagen fan-housing. The ducted air supply was supposed to keep the engine cool enough without the need for a fan. The idea was a miserable failure and, following the demise of five 25bhp engines, the engine compartment lid was redesigned and a conventional cooling system installed. Although it has often been suggested to the contrary, only a Volkswagen engine was fitted to the car in these early days.

The cabriolet was first owned by Kurt Debrunner, marketing manager of AMAG, the Swiss VW importer, who offered 11,500 Swiss Francs for the car in 1950 after seeing it on display in Waibel's showroom. Later, it was owned by Karl Schonbacher, a motorcycle dealer in Pfaffikon. By this time the recorded mileage was in the region of 59,000km.

In July 1975, records show that a duplicate was made of the registration documents, possibly prior to the Waibel being sold to the USA. Michael Rizzuto in California sold the car in 1988 to the present owner, Monty Montgomery of Atlanta, Georgia, via Robert DeMars Ltd of Oakland, California. A total restoration

of the cabriolet was completed in 1992 by Hill and Vaughn.

At this late stage in the vehicle's history, mystery still surrounded the true origins of the Waibel. Hans Waibel himself always insisted that all he had built was a Volkswagen-based special, but even as late as 1986 the Porsche factory hinted at this being an early custom-built 356! The truth is that the Waibel is a Volkswagen-based one-off with engine and chassis numbers that conclusively bear this out. Perhaps the Porsche mystique had clouded people's judgement over the years.

But what of the car itself? It is indeed a pretty aluminium-bodied two-seater, with suicide doors featuring early VW pull-type door handles. The front grille – from a Morris of all things – and the fender skirts on the rear give the cabriolet an American feel, while the specially-made (by Securit) wraparound windscreen and generally rounded lines helped fuel the Porsche argument – although Porsche did not in fact fit curved windscreens to production models until 1953.

Inside the car, the dashboard featured gauges from EBO as fitted by Beutler to the early 356 cabriolets. These consisted of a speedometer, oil temperature and pressure gauges and a voltmeter. The seats were trimmed in leather in a shade of green that complimented the metallic green paintwork, and the folding convertible top was of beige canvas.

The mythical Porsche connection rears its head once again with the 1950/51 Volkswagen-based special known affectionately as 'Ugly' or 'The Pearl'. Little is known of the history of this car, but its present

The 1951 Cryns coupé was inspired by the contemporary Buick Le Sabre, a car considered to be very futuristic at the time. Note the Beetle headlights.

owner, Phil Topcik of Jacksonville, Florida, is constantly searching for more information. 'Ugly' was purchased from friend Ray Novotny, who had originally acquired the car in the mid-'60s for its non-synchromesh transmission. Fortunately he did not dismantle the car as first planned.

Phil Topcik contacted both the Volkswagen and Porsche factories for information on the vehicle, receiving a short reply from the former to the effect that this was not a Volkswagen! The latter, perhaps seduced by the 356-like front end, suggested that it may indeed have been an early Porsche prototype.

The basis of the vehicle is in fact the chassis of a February 1950 VW Beetle, a standard model with mechanical brakes. Onto this has been built a professionally-crafted aluminium body supported by a frame of steel and hardwood. Two small rear-hinged doors give access to the cramped interior. A removable hardtop is fitted, secured by clips above the two-piece windscreen.

The most peculiar aspect of the styling is the long rear deck, featuring two luggage hatches and a strange bulge designed to clear the fan housing of the Volkswagen engine. The 1943 Kübelwagen engine (number 2-030 596) which was originally fitted has long since disappeared. Interestingly enough, the bumpers fitted are identical to those used by Drews in the construction of its own sports car. Inside 'Ugly', the dashboard housed simply a speedometer, a radio and, offset to the passenger side, a grille (with after-market clock) as used in Beetles from 1953 to 1957.

The seats were originally trimmed in red leather, as were the door panels.

'Ugly' is certainly an unusual vehicle, and one whose history is open to conjecture. Could it have been the work of students at one of the many *Karosseriebauschulen* (schools for automobile design)? Or was it the work of an eccentric enthusiast? Recent research suggests it may have been built for a film – but if so, by whom?

Another unusual and equally mysterious special came to light in the Black Forest area of Germany. Towards the end of the 1940s, an automobile enthusiast decided that it would be fun to commission a VW-based sports car from a local coachbuilder in Freiburg. He purchased a Volkswagen chassis, complete with its mechanical brakes and non-synchromesh gearbox, and a 1947 engine, to enable the project to begin. The aluminium body again resembled that of a 356 Porsche, but was in fact approximately 50cm longer due to the provision of modest luggage space behind the engine. The Porsche flavour was further enhanced by the use of certain parts from the 356, including both doors and the fuel tank.

Regrettably, the company chosen to carry out the work did not prove to be the most reliable, and progress was slow. Indeed the bodywork was never completed. Although the craftsman responsible was undeniably a genius at his work, he was a poor manager and his company folded.

The owner of the incomplete vehicle took it home and placed it in storage for several years. He later attempted to finish the job himself, and in doing so modified one front wing to accept a Mercedes 300 headlight unit, giving the car a somewhat lopsided appearance. Today the car remains yet another unique piece of VW lore awaiting its final glory.

Belgium was home to a pair of Volkswagen-based cars in the early 1950s, created by the Cryns coach-

The Stoll coupé was commissioned in 1952 and eventually completed two years later. It remains one of the prettiest conversions ever carried out.

Interior of the Stoll was nicely finished. It was a full four seater.

work concern of Antwerp. Cryns was founded in 1944 and the majority of the work carried out was the final painting, or upholstering, of imported cars of all makes, many of which were delivered in unfinished form. Cryns also specialized in repainting the rather austere post-war Beetles that were sold by the Volkswagen dealership situated across the road.

Familiarity with the Beetle led Cryns to appreciate the suitability of the Volkswagen chassis as the starting point for a coachbuilding project. In 1951, a CKD Deluxe Beetle was acquired with which to begin the task. A steel frame was made to establish the lines of the new body, and then Marcel de Ley, an expert coachbuilder, formed the outer skin from sheet. In all, some twenty sheets of steel, each measuring 2m² ×

A photograph taken outside the original owner's home in the 1950s. The Stoll has changed little over the years.

2mm thick, were used to make the body, although there was considerable wastage due to the one-off nature of the project.

The Cryns incorporated a few parts from vehicles other than a Volkswagen – for example, the door handles were from a Simca Sport – but on the whole, a Beetle provided most of the raw material. An exception was the windscreen, which was a two-piece design intended to keep costs to a minimum.

The engine was a standard air-cooled flat-four, equipped with a modified air-filter that reduced intake noise. Air was drawn into the engine bay via a double-skinned section of bodywork ahead of the motor. Initial testing brought to light an overheating problem, but this was cured following some minor modifications to the engine lid.

Inside the Cryns, the controls were pure Volkswagen, with the exception of the steering wheel which was an aftermarket fitment. As there were no running boards, the body was 30cm/11.8in wider than that of a Beetle, allowing considerably more space for the occupants. Altogether the Cryns was some 20cm/7.9in lower and 8cm/3.1in longer than the car on which it was based. The exterior was finished in two-tone light and dark grey, and the styling was evidently inspired by the 1951 Buick Le Sabre which, at the time, was considered to be a very futuristic car.

Cryns decided to build a second car based on the experience gained from the first sport coupé. This used a wrecked 1953 oval window Beetle as a starting point and differed from the earlier design by incorporating a grille in the engine lid, a curved windscreen and a Golde sun-roof (Cryns was an official Golde agent at the time). Like the first design, this car featured a dummy grille at the front, but the paint finish this time was white with deep red side-panels.

Both of the Cryns were sold to clients, the first car to an engineer in Mechelen, and the second to an unknown client who subsequently modified the car. It is unclear whether either example exists today.

One vehicle of which considerably more is known is the very attractive Stoll coupé currently owned by Bob Shaill of St Leonards on Sea in England. The story begins in 1952 when Herr Bernard Reipenhausen began the search for a new car. His original plan had been to own a Hebmüller, but the demise of that concern following a disastrous fire in July 1949 forced him to look elsewhere. He finally approached Karosserie Stoll GmbH, Bad Nauheim, about the possibility of building a special Volkswagen.

On September 15th 1952, Beetle chassis number 1-0 391 065 left the production line and was subsequently delivered to Autohaus Sheller in Bad Nauheim. From there, the VW made its way to Karosserie Stoll in readiness for an extensive rebuild.

The Beetle underwent considerable surgery over a two-year period to transform it from a regular saloon model into a unique four-seater coupé, superficially similar in appearance to the ill-fated Hebmüller coupé prototype. In detail, the Stoll differed in a number of ways, including the treatment of the rear window which was much larger than that of the Hebmüller and is believed to have been a cut-down BMW 501 glass. Other differences include the shape of the louvres in the rear deck and the lines of the roof.

At the rear, where the Hebmüller models had purpose-made engine lids, the Stoll features an expertly reshaped original Volkswagen panel that has been cut, reformed and rewelded to match the flowing lines of the coupé. To allow it to fit under this new lid, the original VW air-filter was relocated to the side of the engine bay.

This unique model remained in the hands of Herr Reipenhausen right up until 1969, when it was sold to two Americans touring Europe. Did they appreciate the coupé's rarity, or was the vehicle purchased simply as a means of transport?

With a mileage of, by now, over 370,000km, the coupé was sold to persons unknown in 1971. Eventually the car arrived in England and was issued with the registration mark EAN 24J. At some point soon after this, the Stoll was stolen, only to reappear in a somewhat derelict state in London. A VW enthusiast purchased the remains, planning to restore the coupé to its former glory, but lost interest when it became clear that the price would be high.

Another enthusiast, Tommy Dobson, stepped in and acquired the car, later selling it to Bob Shaill who proceeded to carry out an extensive restoration over a period of no less than fourteen years! The end result is breathtaking: two-tone beige over ivory paintwork (the original colours were beige over grey) and tan leather upholstery make this historically important Volkswagen derivative extremely attractive.

By way of a complete contrast, the brainchild of Jacques Ladyjensky in 1955 was neither especially attractive nor the fruit of a metal-crafter's labours. Based on a 1954 chassis, the Ladyjensky roadster was a simple two-seater moulded in glassfibre (GRP), then a new material.

Initially it was the military which showed most interest in GRP, and it was not really until 1947 that the general public became fully aware of the advantages of the material. Although many companies such as Chrysler in 1946 and Austin in 1950 had experimented with GRP as a material suitable for the manufacture of automobile bodies, it wasn't until 1953 that Chevrolet took the bull by the horns and produced the world's first mass-produced GRP-bodied car, the Corvette.

Jacques Ladyjensky, a student of civil engineering, presented his prototype body based on a VW chassis two years later. Weighing a modest 80kg, the bodyshell was moulded by the Belgian Solvay company. As a result of this connection, Ladyjensky was asked to exhibit his completed vehicle at the 1957 International Car Fair in Brussels where it attracted much interest from King Baudouin of Belgium. Regrettably, this interest was not shared by the Volkswagen factory, which firmly believed that the only true way ahead lay with the Beetle or the stylish – and expensive – Karmann Ghia.

Later in his career, the creator of this roadster went on to help with the construction of the famous Atomium building, part of the World Expo at Brussels in 1958 and used as a museum until the present day. Sadly the Ladyjensky car does not survive: it failed the stringent annual Belgian technical inspection after 150,000km of use and was scrapped.

In similar vein is the eminently practical sedan built for his own personal use by Mr Mechyr, an employee of the Czechoslovakian company Karosserie Sodomka.

The Ladyjensky was one of the earliest of the glassfibre-bodied specials. Created in 1955 on a 1954 chassis, the roadster was driven for 150,000km.

The Sodomka saloon (left) was another glass-fibre-bodied car. Built in Czechoslovakia on a Type 82 Kübelwagen chassis, the Sodomka owes its styling to the Wartburg 311.

For many years the car on the right was identified as a Karmann Ghia-based model, but subsequent research suggests that it is another Beetle-derived coupé.

Also using the latest GRP technology, Mechyr commenced work on a car of his own design using the ubiquitous Type 82 Kübelwagen chassis as a starting point. Apparently influenced by the popular Wartburg 311 saloon, the lines of the Sodomka special have stood the test of time well – a tribute to the restraint shown by Mr Mechyr at a time when many others seemed intent on building a vision of the car of the future.

Although originally fitted with the Kübelwagen engine, the car was later equipped with a more modern 34bhp 1192cc unit. Aside from that, much of the car is as originally built back in the 1950s. It is still in use today, is in generally very good condition and has covered in excess of 300,000km.

A vehicle that has had many guessing at its origins is a stylish coupé that initially appears to be derived from a Karmann Ghia. The coupé is a noteworthy for its very low waistline, deeply contoured sides, heavy air vents in the rear wings and a reverse-angled panoramic rear window.

Inside the car, a folding rear seat from a Beetle is used, and despite the slightly limited headroom the vehicle evidently aimed to be a full four-seater. The dashboard owed more to American styling of the era, with sweeping lines and an instrument binnacle in front of the driver. A small glove box could be found in front of the passenger.

From certain angles the styling was not dissimilar to the later Renault Floride coupé, yet this was no product of a major manufacturer. Built in 1955 and originating from the former East Germany, this coupé remains something of a mystery. Does it still exist?

As was commonplace in such seats of learning, towards the end of the 1950s the students of the *Karosseriebauschule* Kaiserslautern were given a project to demonstrate the skills they had each learned at the school. According to Herr Franz Spies, a master student at the time, a class of between 20 and 25 master students was divided into groups of five or six and, working from a set of accurate drawings, each was responsible for making a different part of the car – the roof, doors, wings etc. This way, it was possible to individually assess the skills of each student.

Now owned by Paul J Craft in the USA, the Kaiserslautern coupé is based on a Volkswagen chassis which left the factory with a Beetle bodyshell on March 19th 1954. Delivered to Schmidt & Kock in Bremen, the export model was most probably damaged in an accident and subsequently purchased by the students as the basis for their project.

Onto the bare chassis the students built a stylish two-seater coupé body which from certain angles owes much to the lines of the Karmann Ghia. Made of steel as opposed to the more commonplace aluminium, the body was made up of several individual panels each hand-formed over wooden bucks, a tedious job that taxed the students' skills to the maximum.

All the ancillary parts such as the lights, windows and instruments were purchased new and sourced from a variety of vehicles. The headlights are those of

a Karmann Ghia, the tail-lights from a Porsche 356, as is the grille in the engine lid. The front windscreen came from a DKW 1000 while the rear window is in fact the front windscreen of a Karmann Ghia coupé. The Karmann Ghia also supplied the front and rear bumpers. A Golde sunroof completes the picture.

On completion, but before final preparation and painting, the body was closely inspected by the examining committee, headed by a Professor Olvermann, and the students' work assessed accordingly.

There are some interesting details, including the fact that the body is considerably wider than the Volkswagen chassis, necessitating the use of box-section outriggers to support the sills. The front seats are mounted further forward and lower to the floor than in a Beetle and the pedal assembly has been inverted so that the pedals hinge from above to gain some extra room. The rear seat is mounted very low, with deep footwells let into the floorpans to allow more space for the passengers' legs.

A simple but effective method was used to create some space in front of the driver's feet whereby the steering box was moved from the upper to the lower torsion beam on the front suspension. The spindle assemblies were then swopped from one side to the other to allow the track rods to pass below the level of the chassis.

The Kaiserslautern coupé remains one of the most impressive one-offs ever created, for rarely does a vehicle created by what amounted to a committee turn out to be so handsome. As an example of the

coachbuilder's art, it remains a fine testimony.

However, handsome is not a word one would readily use to describe the coupé designed and built by Georg Erdmann towards the end of the 1950s. Erdmann was a craftsman, learning his panel-beating skills during the 1930s at Dörr & Schreck, a coach-building concern in Frankfurt established in 1919. Dörr & Schreck was well respected for its aerodynamic designs penned by Baron von Koenig-Fachsenfeld, using Maybach chassis in particular.

A period of almost twenty years was then spent in the employ of Autenreith in Darmstadt, another much respected concern with close connections with BMW, following which Erdmann decided to set up in business himself, also at Darmstadt. Initially his company concentrated on repairs and rebuilds, but eventually, as is so often the case, Erdmann decided that he too should prove his capabilities by creating a vehicle to his own design.

In 1957 he purchased a new Volkswagen chassis, complete with running gear, and set about designing a somewhat over-styled four-seater coupé. The lines were fairly typical of an era when there was much debate over what cars of the future would look like. The end result was, by all accounts, clearly inspired by American cars of the mid-fifties – notably Buick with its sweeping side trim and pinched waistline. The front end, however, defied comparison with any make or model regardless of country of origin.

The wraparound windscreen was 'borrowed' from an Opel Rekord, while the rear screen was that of a

The Kaiserslautern coupé was built by a coachbuilding school in Germany on the chassis of a 1954 Beetle. The car is considerably longer than a VW.

At the rear, lights and an intake grille from a Porsche 356 have been fitted. Note the long rear overhang.

Goliath Hansa 1100. A Taunus 15M gave up its tail-lights, which were positioned at the base of some quite extraordinary fins on the rear wings. Much of the chrome decor was pirated from an Opel, although the heavily styled frontal trim, incorporating a central driving lamp, was of Erdmann's own creation.

The majority of the body was formed out of steel, although in an effort to save weight and to aid manufacture, the doors and front and rear lids were of aluminium. However, despite these weight savings, the Erdmann coupé proved to be 30kg/66lb heavier than the export model Beetle on which it was based. With a standard 30bhp Volkswagen engine in the rear, performance could hardly have been electrifying.

The coupé was equipped with four seats, the rear being fairly short on legroom. The seats were trimmed in modern synthetic materials, as were the side panels, and the dashboard housed the basic Beetle instruments.

The car eventually saw the light of day on August 5th 1960 following almost three years of work. The stringent official examination of the vehicle prior to its

being used on the road gave the car a clean bill of health. Georg Erdmann used his coupé regularly until the end of 1967 when it was taken off the road.

Subsequent examinations by the official German test authorities, the TUV, have resulted in concern being shown over those rear fins. At some point in the recent past, one of these fins has been taken away, and an attempt made to remove the other. However, it is the aim of the current owner, Horst Hilberseimer of Augsburg, to restore the coupé to its original befinned glory.

At first sight, the intriguing Moto-Torino roadster appears to be some sort of kit as marketed today by a number of companies across the world enabling a regular Volkswagen saloon to be converted into a Hebmüller-like roadster. Closer examination, however, reveals a different story.

Despite much research, the Moto-Torino remains something of a mystery – nobody knows how many were built or who commissioned them. These questions may never be answered as the Moto-Torino workshops are no longer in existence.

The Ghia 'Aigle' was a styling exercise by SpA Ghia of Turin. Built in 1957, the stubby yet elegant coupé failed to attract the attention of Wolfsburg.

The example seen here began life as a regular saloon in August 1959. Soon after, it was delivered to Moto-Torino in Turin for conversion, and then delivered back to Germany. The roadster was then serviced by the Glockler VW dealership prior to exportation to Florida in 1960.

Examining the car, it is clear that this is the product of a skilled coachbuilder, utilizing as it does many new VW cabriolet body panels, including the windscreen surround. Other parts to complete the conversion were purpose made by Moto-Torino.

The rear deck of the car is perhaps the least visually pleasing aspect of the conversion, having a slightly humped appearance due to the fact that the original – although much modified – engine lid is used. Powered by the standard 30bhp engine, the Moto-Torino roadster may have been a unique vehicle – or perhaps not, for a period photograph of another roadster taken in Belgium during the 1960s suggests that it is possible Moto-Torino did in fact carry out a similar conversion at an earlier point in time. Although based on what is believed to be a 1956 or 1957 model, the Belgian vehicle is remarkably similar in many ways to the later car. The principal differences are the shape of the engine lid at its top edge, and the form of the side windows. However, this second roadster remains unattributed to another company and may indeed be a product of the Moto-Torino concern.

When in the late 1950s it became obvious that Volkswagen would have to begin to look at an alternative to the Beetle at some point in the future, a game of rumour and counter-rumour began in the motoring press. Eventually, of course, the speculation came to an end when Volkswagen launched its Type 3 range in 1961, with the so-called 'Notchback' being the likely Beetle replacement.

However, many styling houses made their own attempts at guessing what the 'Beetle' of the future might look like. Among the best-known, of course, is Ghia of Turin which produced a one-off styling exercise called the Ghia Aigle in 1957. Based on a contem-

The Moto-Torino does not have the elegant lines of a Hebmüller but is still an attractive car. The roadster dates back to 1959, when it was built in Turin.

porary Beetle, the Aigle was a somewhat stubby coupé with smooth, flowing lines and simple trim – apart from some rather grotesque fake 'wire' wheel covers.

The Aigle was an elegant car, obviously well-executed by one of the most famous – and talented – styling houses of all time. However, Ghia was not alone in its endeavours to improve the breed.

A Mr Guglielmetti of Geneva ran a small company by the name of Italsuisse and in 1960 he launched his version of the VW that could have been, choosing the Geneva Motor Show to display his creation. Starting with a regular Beetle chassis, Italsuisse built a crisply-lined, if uninspiring, two-door saloon powered by the ubiquitous 30bhp engine. Serious in his intentions to sell his design to the factory, Guglielmetti made a point of using as many VW parts as possible in his design, and even, it is said, went as far as forming the body panels from the same gauge material as used by

The Erdmann has a very organic feel to it, with its flowing lines and art deco-like trim. The central headlight unit helps give a futuristic look.

Originally fitted with a pair of fins, the Erdmann has suffered the indignity of being 'legalized' for use on German roads. The present owner plans to refit the fins.

Volkswagen so that the ride characteristics would be similar to those of a Beetle.

Although some 50mm/2in longer and 150mm/6in lower than a Beetle, the car remained a full four-seater, with access to the rear via tilting front seats. Interior space, despite the altered roof line, remained good, largely due to the specially-made seats being lower than the originals. Dashboard features included Karmann Ghia gauges, the ashtray from a 1950s Beetle, a VW steering wheel and a radio blanking panel, again from an oval-window VW.

Externally, the Italsuisse Volkswagen was restrained in its trim, chrome bumpers and window surrounds being about as far as Guglielmetti dare go if the design was to be accepted by the Wolfsburg hierarchy. However, the body did feature a rather avant-garde treatment of both front and rear lighting, the former consisting of dual headlights from a Fiat 2100, the latter high-level units mounted sideways on the top corners of the wings.

Sadly for Italsuisse, the project was not worth the effort, for Volkswagen had already made up its mind

about a new car long before this proposal saw the light of day. It is written that Guglielmetti threatened to drop his body onto a DKW chassis and challenge the new VW head on, but history proves it to have been an empty threat.

Although the Italsuisse saloon was fully intended to be the first of a production series, it remained the only one of its kind – a costly reminder that challenging the big boys on their home territory could be a fruitless task.

Finally, there remains the ABR. Built in 1960 by a talented blacksmith called Alfons Booren in Belgium and based on a 1958 Beetle chassis, the ABR was a steel-bodied two-seater powered by a Porsche 356 engine. It was unusual for its day by having rear body-work that hinged rearward in one piece to give excellent access to the engine and drivetrain. The front bodywork similarly hinged forward for access to the Beetle fuel tank and spare wheel.

The running gear was all VW with the exception of the brakes, which were Porsche 356 in origin. Later, the Beetle wheels were crudely widened, with

Another attempt by an Italian styling studio to provide Volkswagen with an alternative to the Beetle was the angular Italsuisse saloon of 1960.

Although somewhat crudely-built, the ABR was definitely ahead of its time in overall styling. Reminiscent of a later Alpine 110, the body is well-proportioned.

The proud owner poses with his masterpiece somewhere in the Belgian countryside. Note how the tops of the ABR's doors were cut into the roof to improve access.

'spokes' welded in place to imitate lightweight racing wheels.

The body was formed of steel sheet, hand-formed over a tubular frame. Access to the interior was via wide, front-hinged doors. Once inside, the occupants sat on home-made seats and were confronted with a dazzling array of instrumentation arranged in a decidedly unergonomic fashion.

For all its apparent crudity, the ABR was a well-built sports car with some ingenious features that were well ahead of their time. Sadly, like so many others its ilk, the ABR was eventually scrapped. All that remain are a few photographs to remind us of the efforts of Alfons Booren.

One can only guess at how many similar specials came and went without being captured on film.

UTILITIES
FROM AMBULANCES TO DELIVERY VANS

From the very beginning, the Volkswagen was seen as a suitable base for utilitarian variations. In wartime, the Beetle chassis found its way, essentially unchanged, under the Type 82 Kübelwagen. During the British occupation of the factory in the immediate post-war period, the Beetle became a van, a pick-up, a warehouse 'donkey' – even the basis for what became the Type 2. Its potential was remarkable, and many came to realize that there was far more to the Beetle than simply a car for the people.

It was during the immediate post-war period when the factory was under the control of the MilGov that Ivan Hirst first exploited the potential of the VW chassis as a basis for a load-carrier. To help with moving components about the factory, Hirst had borrowed some fork lift trucks from the British Army. However, after a short while the Army HQ decided that the trucks were needed elsewhere. Immediately, the German supervisors threw their hands up in horror and demanded of Hirst how they would be able to carry on work without them.

Hirst made the simple suggestion that they take a Beetle chassis, mount a seat above the engine, a flat platform across the floorpan and steer it using a long drag link running from the steering box back to the rear-mounted steering column. A number of these 'donkeys' were built, some reportedly still in use up until recent times.

Ben Pon, the Dutchman who became the first official VW export agent, saw these workhorses and sketched out his ideas for a proper commercial vehicle based on VW components. This eventually led to the construction of what became known as the Type 2, but not before some extensive testing had proved that the basic Beetle floorpan was not up to the task of carrying a large load, having literally collapsed under the strain.

Outside the factory, one of the first private conversions for business use was that carried out by the local Volkswagen dealer in Wolfsburg, Schwen. In 1947, this company converted a Beetle into a useful, if not stylish, delivery van. The conversion was simple, with

This 1947 delivery van was built and used by a local dealer, Schwen, in Wolfsburg in connection with his business. Note the external Kübelwagen-style semaphore indicators.

The Hebmüller Type 18A was a rather crude conversion to make the Beetle saloon into something more applicable to the role of Police car.

new rear quarter panels extending back from the door pillars to form a seemingly cavernous loading area above the engine. A pair of side-hinged rear doors gave access to both engine and load.

Among the unusual features of this particular van – and it makes an interesting comparison with the later conversion by Beutler (whose vehicles are covered in detail in a later chapter) – are the retention of the original saloon side window and the rear wings which have been extensively reshaped. Also of note are the Kübelwagen-style semaphore indicators mounted on the front quarter panels. This is particularly interesting as there is no reason why the conversion from saloon to van should have necessitated the removal of the original semaphores from the door pillars.

This restored Hebmüller Type 18A is one of the rare models with steel doors in place of the more usual canvas side-screens.

A Parisian baker built this rather austere-looking delivery wagon. It is based on a 1946 or 1947 Beetle and uses a steel-skinned body over a wooden frame.

The Topinette camping car conversion could be built at home with regular hand tools. It may not have been very elegant, but it was adequate for a weekend away.

On the rear of the Schwen conversion were two tiny windows which could have given the driver only the most limited of views of the road behind. Lower down, a pair of vents – one in each door – provided cooling air for the engine. There was only one rear light, and no rear bumper was fitted to the vehicle. Unfortunately, the Schwen van no longer exists.

By way of contrast, in the early 1950s a Parisian baker decided to convert a Beetle into a delivery wagon. Based on a 1946 or 1947 model, the vehicle (which still survives though in extremely poor condition) was equipped with a voluminous station wagon body built using a steel-skinned wooden frame. The roof was made from wooden slats covered in fabric. At present, nothing more is known of the history of this wagon, which currently awaits restoration.

Another French oddity is the 1952 Topinette. This was a camping conversion using the front half of the Beetle saloon combined with a wood-framed rear in which the occupants could sleep. Access to the sleeping accommodation was via a side door, while a second door, or tailgate, was fitted to the rear above the engine bay. The conversion was extremely simple, anything but elegant, but evidently practical in its design. The Topinette was available as either a factory-fitted or a do-it-yourself conversion.

By far the most interesting utility Volkswagens were the Police models produced by Hebmüller, Papler and Austro-Tatra.

Hebmüller, which has its own chapter later in the book, built a prototype based on a cut-down 1947 Beetle. This still retained the saloon windscreen surround, which looked somewhat heavy on a convertible model. The biggest problem, in common with every convertible conversion on a regular saloon, was chassis flex. At first this was tackled with the addition of deep box-section strengtheners welded around the heater channels and sills. Although this cured the problem to a degree, it was not fully solved until under-sill strengthening rails were added to the production models. These rails meant that the strengthening sections across the door openings could be reduced in height, thus facilitating entry and exit. The other principal modification made to the production models was the use of a Karmann-style squared-off windscreen surround, which greatly improved both appearance and visibility.

In service, the main drawback with the Hebmüller Police car was the fact that it was not a true all-weather vehicle. The majority of the Type 18A models, as they became designated, were equipped only with canvas 'doors', and ropes, to prevent the rain from getting in – or the occupants from falling out. There was also a pair of rather inadequate wind-wings either side of the windscreen. Aside from that, there was no other weather protection. With the hood raised, the doors and sidescreens in place and the wind-wings attached, there was no guarantee that the occupants would remain dry in anything but the lightest of April showers. Hebmüller addressed this problem to some extent by building a few of the Police models with steel doors and these, when fitted with their sidescreens, offered considerably better protection from the elements.

First built in 1947, the Type 18A Hebmüller required a lot of strengthening to retain an acceptable degree of rigidity. Note the wind wings. The canvas 'doors' offered little protection to the occupants in anything but the lightest of showers. The folding roof was very loose fitting.

Hand rails were attached to the seats and door openings. Note the exposed hood frame behind the rear door.

Inside the Type 18A, the controls and seating were all as per the Standard model Beetle, with black dashboard fittings and a simple black three-spoke steering wheel. All the Police models were painted dark green, in either matt or semi-gloss finish according to usage. Everything, including the hubcaps, headlight surrounds and grooved bumpers, was treated to the same dark green. Being based on Standard model saloons, they were all equipped with cable brakes.

Hebmüller built its Type 18A models from 1948 to 1952, starting with the body number 18.00000. Unfortunately there is no record of how many were made, and quite how many survive is also unknown. Only one steel-door version is known today, along with just a handful of canvas-door models.

Cologne-based Papler was well known in coachbuilding circles as being responsible for the production of some extremely elegant vehicles based on the chassis of Rolls-Royce and Mercedes motorcars prior to the Second World war. Founded in 1908 by Franz Papler, the *Karosserie* could name many of the major manufacturers among its clients, including Ford, Adler and Minerva. After the war, however, there was less demand for such works of coachbuilding art, and attention turned more and more towards working vehicles, including Police models based on the Volkswagen Beetle.

In 1950, as well as converting Ford saloons, Papler built its first Volkswagen-based four-door Police car. Unfortunately the firm did not benefit from official factory support like Hebmüller, so all the necessary Beetles had to be purchased from a variety of sources,

and thus all Paplers still retained the original Wolfsburg body numbers.

When a comparison is made between a Papler and a Hebmüller Type 18A, there are immediately a number of differences. On the Papler, for instance, the hood was a very much better designed affair, with all the framework concealed behind the fabric. Also, and more significantly, all Papler versions featured steel doors, these being better thought out than those fitted by Hebmüller.

Although the Papler was converted from a Beetle saloon, the windscreen glass used was the same as that of the Karmann cabriolet model, with its squared-off corners. However, the windscreen surround was

The Papler Type 18A Police car (left) bene-fited from a better-designed folding roof – and steel doors. Note the externally-mounted semaphore indicators.

Some Type 18As were purchased by the fire department. This recently-seen Papler (above) has been fitted with incorrect rear lights and hubcaps. Note cabrio engine cover.

considerably thicker than that of the regular cabriolet model or the Hebmüller version.

All Paplers sold to the Police were finished in dark green, while a few examples used by the fire department were painted red. Exactly how many were built is not known, and only three or maybe four are known to have survived.

The third Police-model Volkswagen was that produced by the Austrian company, Austro-Tatra. Also designated the Type 18A, the Austro-Tatra Beetle first appeared in 1950, the Vienna Police

placing an order for 150. The business was handled by Porsche Konstruktionen GmbH, latterly known as Porsche GmbH & Co, in Salzburg, sole Volkswagen importers for the whole of Austria.

The Austro-Tatra Type 18As shared many attributes of the two other Police variants, but not necessarily the better ones. They came with the partly-exposed hood frame that was a less attractive feature of the Hebmüller version, and steel doors that were not as well executed as those of the Papler. A lack of strength was the main drawback.

Some changes were made to the basic design during production. For example, the air intake louvres normally found beneath the rear window of a saloon model were in some cases left as part of the main body, and in others incorporated into the engine lid. Another variation that could be found between different models was that on some the front doors were much wider than those at the rear, presumably

All dressed up and no place to go. Local police officers pose for an official photograph – note how the rear passengers sit higher in this Austro-Tatra Type 18A.

With Police sirens, extra spot lights, twin horns and sunvisors, this line-up of Austro-Tatras is an accessory hunter's delight!

where access to the rear seat was considered to be of less importance.

Of the 203 Austro-Tatra Type 18As believed to have been built, all were supplied for use by the Austrian Police and only a handful are thought to have survived. However, one of these has the body number 18.00319 which, if the numbering began at 18.00000, would suggest that at least 319 examples were built, not 203! Unfortunately no accurate records were kept, so once again no one will ever really know the true figure.

One of the more unlikely uses to which the ever-versatile Beetle was put was in the rôle of ambulance.

Certainly the British military command had foreseen a demand for such vehicles, and had indeed designated a model number – Type 83 – accordingly, but that was little more than a box mounted on the back of a cut-down saloon.

Miesen, a coachbuilding company founded in Bonn in 1870, however, saw the Beetle ambulance taking on an altogether different form: a saloon car with the ability to carry a patient and stretcher alongside the driver. That Miesen was interested in producing an ambulance came as no surprise, for although the company's roots lay in carriage-building, horse-drawn ambulances were first produced by them as early as 1901, motorized versions following four years later.

During the Second World War Miesen converted its first Volkswagen model, a Type 82E – the Kübelwagen-chassised Beetle – for use as an ambulance. Immediately after the war this work continued, producing ambulances for the occupying forces and, later, for such organizations as the Red Cross. Initially the Type 51 chassis was used, this being technically identical to the wartime Type 82E, but then the Type 11 (later known simply as the Type 1) regular chassis was favoured. In total, 150 of these basic ambulances were built under British control.

The Miesen ambulance was given the official

The Miesen Krankenwagen, or ambulance, was an interesting conversion first produced during the war. The post-war version seen here saw use in Wolfsburg.

The patient on his stretcher was loaded onto a platform which could be swivelled round into the car alongside the driver. The door was modified so that it could open wider.

model number of Type 17, and was listed as costing just DM900 more than the normal saloon model. Conversion took approximately four weeks from the time of order, occasionally longer if a more complex specification was demanded.

For a Beetle saloon to be able to carry an adult on a stretcher, and still be capable of being driven, required some careful planning on Miesen's part. The front passenger seat and rear seats were removed, to be replaced by specially-designed folding units. These could be folded down to form a flat surface onto which a swivelling platform was then fitted. The patient and stretcher could be slid onto this platform and then guided into the vehicle along runners, before being carefully swivelled round to tuck inside the Beetle body. Clearly, this would require a degree of care on the part of the ambulance personnel for fear of further injuring the patient!

To help with the conversion, the gear lever was dog-legged towards the driver, and the rear seat back–

rest was split into two so that once the stretcher was in place a passenger could be carried alongside the patient. A further modification was made to the passenger door hinges, allowing the door to swing back against the front wing, which was itself slightly reshaped accordingly.

To help the patient remain comfortable on the journey to hospital, a pad was mounted on the bulkhead panel below the rear windscreen to protect his head. A small pair of steps was incorporated into the running board to facilitate entry and exit. On the roof, a wooden drop-sided box was fitted in which the stretcher was normally stowed, along with all the other hardware associated with ambulance duties, such as blankets, first-aid box and the like.

In all, it is believed that approximately 500 of these ingenious vehicles were delivered, the last of them as recently as the early 1960s. Surely there cannot be a better way for a Volkswagen enthusiast to take a trip

The Meeussen station wagon was a well-proportioned conversion. Note the cooling louvres in the rear quarter panels and the side-hinged rear door.

to hospital than in a Beetle ambulance?

Finally, there is the attractive series of six 'estate car' conversions carried out by the Belgian company of Meeussen. Very similar to the contemporary conversion by Beutler, the Meeussen differs in that the cooling air for the standard Beetle engine is drawn in through louvres in the quarter panels behind the rear wheels. Another feature unique to the Meeussen was the side-hinged tailgate, which swung open to give access to both the engine and rear load area at the same time. This was in fact made out of the right hand door of a Beetle! The majority of the bodywork was original Beetle, but the roof and rear side panels were new. The rear wings were modified saloon panels, while the rear bumper is of unknown origin.

KARMANN
THE FIRST WITH FACTORY APPROVAL

The name Karmann evokes images of Volkswagen cabriolets and coupés. In Volkswagen circles one has only to mention the word 'cabrio' and inevitably the picture of a Karmann-built convertible Beetle springs to mind. But Karmann GmbH began life in the same way as so many other coachbuilding companies in Germany, by constructing horse-drawn carriages towards the close of the last century.

Founded in 1874, the family business carried out its first commission on a motor car in 1902 for Dürkopp. One year later, Karmann made the decision to concentrate on this evidently lucrative – and certainly growing – sector of the coachbuilding market. He acquired the Klages carriageworks in Osnabrück and, with a staff of eight, accepted commissions from a number of companies. The first of these was AGA which ordered 1000 bodies, a very sizeable commission in those early days.

Then began a long and profitable relationship with Adler, during which many beautiful cabriolets were built on a variety of chassis. The Adler Autobahn

model saw Karmann make the first step towards producing all-steel bodywork, following a visit to the USA where the latest press tooling was in regular use.

Sadly, the success was relatively short-lived, for the depression of the late 1920s in Germany saw the demise of many old established names in the automobile industry. Companies such as Hansa-Lloyd, who had been good customers of Karmann, disappeared, never to be seen again. It was only the links with Adler that kept Karmann alive.

By the outbreak of the Second World War Karmann GmbH employed 600 people, but disaster was about to strike. During the war, the Karmann works were severely damaged by Allied bombing, rendering any coachbuilding work impossible. Instead, on cessation of hostilities, the workforce began producing the essentials of any post-war economy. Such unglamorous products as wheelbarrows, cutlery and folding chairs took the place of stylish cabriolets for the rich and famous, but with the gradual return to production of the Volkswagen, Karmann's interest in

The 1949 cabriolet in almost its final form ready for production. However, there are no semaphore indicators fitted – Karmann had still not made up its mind about position.

The rear view of this beautiful 1951 model clearly shows the louvres pressed into the engine lid for cooling. Note that there are no louvres below the window.

The 1951 Karmann cabriolet had all of the features introduced that year on the regular saloon models, including the characteristic vents in the front quarter panels.

coachbuilding was rekindled. The problem was that, as a German citizen, Wilhelm Karmann was not able to obtain a Beetle, except with an official permit. Worse still, the coachworks were only allowed to carry out essential repair work, not body-making.

Eventually, after much perseverance, Karmann was finally given a Beetle at no cost – the 10,000th to be built after the war, dated November 1946. Soon a second vehicle was made available. But why the sudden change of heart?

During the British occupation of the Wolfsburg factory, there had been talk of the possibility of building a cabriolet version of the Beetle. Indeed, as we have seen, the British had already built at least two open-topped Beetles, a two-seater as used by Charles Radclyffe, and a four-seater used by Ivan Hirst. After

The first publicity photograph from 1949 shows an interesting vehicle. It has been hastily built using KdF-Wagen front wings, and the fit of the doors is not good.

An excellent overall view of a 1955 model. The semaphores have now moved to their customary position behind the doors. The large hood bag was a standard feature.

the war, both Karmann and Hebmüller visited the factory and discussed their plans, and both were given the go-ahead to develop cabriolet prototypes.

Within a very short space of time, two prototypes were built by Karmann, the first with only wind-down door windows, external hood hinges and no rear windscreen at all. The second had the more familiar wind-down rear side windows and concealed hinges. The main problem, in common with the Hebmüller design, was flexing. Despite the Beetle having a separate chassis with a substantial backbone, when the roof was cut off the body and chassis would flex badly.

Karmann ultimately solved the problem with strengthening members under each sill, redesigned front quarter panels and reinforcement round the door openings. The main drawback of this reinforcement was an increase in weight to around 770kg/1700lb, approximately 40kg/88lb more than a Beetle saloon,

so with the standard Volkswagen engine the cabriolet lost out slightly in performance terms.

Despite the success of the prototypes, any thoughts of series production were dashed for the time being due to the post-war shortage of raw materials such as sheet steel and suitable fabric for the roof. Not until the sweeping financial reforms of June 1948 did production look feasible as materials once again became available.

Wolfsburg had been placed in the care of Heinz Nordhoff, the new General Manager since January 1948, and it was he who approved further develop-ment by Karmann of the cabriolet. A third prototype was produced in May 1949, this being very similar to the second example of 1946, followed soon after by a series of 25 pre-production models. These were subjected to an extensive test programme of over 20,000km, which was concluded on August 5th by a report that stated how favourably impressed the factory

A Police model from 1950. Note the matt paint and the tyre pressures stencilled onto each wing. A lack of chrome trim is also apparent.

By 1959, the lines of the Beetle had changed considerably. The louvres in the engine cover of all cabrio models were now very different in form.

was with the Karmann cabriolet. Later that month Nordhoff gave Karmann an order for the first batch of 2000 cars, the only stipulation being that original Volkswagen components should be used wherever possible.

Karmann took Beetles from Wolfsburg and sliced them off at the waistline. New panels were then grafted on to complete the transformation. In production terms, the arrangement worked perfectly, even if Wolfsburg did insist on a lot of paperwork, carefully defining deliveries of every component to Osnabrück.

With a works number of VW Type 15, the

Karmann cabriolet went into full production in 1949, starting with one or two cars per day in September and rising to six per day in December. By the end of the year a total of 364 examples had been completed. The rate of production began to rise steadily, the 1000th car leaving the works in April 1950. In February an order had been received for an extra 2000 cars, and by the end of that year a further 2695 cabriolets had been built. The convertible Beetle was on its way.

Over the following years the design remained essentially unchanged, save for the adoption of any improvements made to the saloon model by Wolfsburg. Production reached its peak (as far as the period covered by this book is concerned) in 1960 with 11,921 units.

In 1952 Karmann assumed responsibility for the production of the last remaining Hebmüller two-seat cabriolets as a result of the problems suffered by that factory following the disastrous fire of 1949, and altogether fifteen Type 14A models were built before production ceased in 1953.

However, Beetle cabriolets were not the only Volkswagen-based vehicles produced by Karmann. Prior to his death in 1951 Wilhelm Karmann had dreamed of building a car from scratch as opposed to simply converting another company's product. His son, Wilhelm Jr, made that dream come true. As early as 1950, Karmann had discussed the idea of a sports convertible with Wolfsburg, but in no conclusive fashion. The discussion continued for the next two or three years while Nordhoff debated the project. The problem was that the Beetle was by now so successful

Karmann has always prided itself on the fit of the folding roof of all its models. With plenty of padding, and a glass rear window, it's as quiet as a saloon.

By the mid-fifties, metallic paint had become popular – and what car does such a finish more justice than a Karmann cabriolet?

that the need for another model in the Volkswagen range was questionable. This line of thought on Nordhoff's part was almost the company's downfall later in the 1950s, when the idea of an eventual replacement for the Beetle was put on the back-burner for far too long.

Nordhoff rejected Karmann's own ideas, so the Osnabrück factory turned to Turin, and Carrozzeria Ghia, for inspiration. Wilhelm Karmann had met Luigi Segre, Commercial Director of Ghia, at motor shows in the past and discussed the idea of a sports coupé with him. Unbeknown to Karmann, Segre decided to go ahead and order a Beetle chassis via Charles LeDouche, the French Volkswagen importer. He chose this route partly because the factory had refused in the past to supply a chassis direct, and partly because he wished to keep the project secret from Karmann.

In 1953 Segre invited Karmann to Paris to view a

new Ghia prototype which had been completed in just five months. The effect was dramatic. Aside from the vehicle being a coupé rather than a convertible, the sporty design was almost exactly what Karmann had had in mind and, after some detail changes had been made, the prototype was shipped off to Osnabrück.

Shortly after, on November 16th, Heinz Nordhoff and Dr Feuereisen (VW's Vice-President in charge of sales) were shown the coupé and gave it their blessing. A number of minor changes were made to aid production, but essentially what Nordhoff and Feuereisen saw was what the public would get.

The changes made to the prototype included widening the floorpan by 80cms, altering the springing, adding a front anti-roll bar, adjusting the angle of the steering column and shortening the gear lever. Although the engine and transmission remained untouched, the air-filter from a Type 2 was fitted due to the low line of the engine lid. The bumpers were slightly redesigned to offer greater protection to the body, and the headlamps were relocated to make them less obtrusive. The familiar fresh-air intakes were also added to the nose. But, interesting to note, none of the advanced features (for the time) such as the frameless door windows, high waistline, cable-operated

Karmann always exploited two-tone paint schemes. Coupés were often seen in striking colour combinations such as this pale yellow and black.

Engine access was always good on a Ghia. The air filter had to be relocated due to the lower body line, but apart from that the engine was unchanged.

Inside, the Ghia was better trimmed than a Beetle. Note the unique dashboard, which owed more to Porsche than Volkswagen.

The prototype Karmann Ghia appeared in 1953 and was greeted enthusiastically by Heinz Nordhoff, Volkswagen's General Manager since 1948. The prototype coupé did not feature the characteristic air intakes on the front panel. The wings were also very much more curved than on production models.

At the rear, a large number of louvres were stamped into the engine lid, along with a pair of stylized vents either side of the licence plate.

bonnet and boot locks, over-centre hinges or push-button doorlocks were questioned. The Karmann Ghia coupé had arrived.

The body was expensive to build, and very labour intensive, for it was truly a hand-built car. There were no large presses at Karmann at this time, and complex panels such as the shapely nose had to be built up out of several smaller panels, each carefully welded to the next. Each body required almost 4m of welding on the outer skin, every seam being filled and finished in lead. By this time over 1700 people were employed at Karmann, and it comes as no surprise that 1000 of them worked in the body shop alone.

The official launch was brought forward to July 14th as space was at a premium in the Karmann factory. At first orders were slow, with just 37 cars delivered to dealers in August, but a display at the Frankfurt Motor Show changed all that, and public demand forced Karmann to speed up production. By the end of the year the 500th coupé had been

produced and, almost unbelievably, the 10,000th example left the line just 14 months later.

The convertible version, which had in fact been built in prototype form back in 1954, went into production on August 1st 1957 at a price of DM8250. The coupé by this time cost DM7500.

Behind the story of the Karmann Ghia there has always been an air of intrigue, for a dispute arose over who really was responsible for the design. One claimant is Virgil Exner, or rather his successors. Exner was the talented stylist who, following an influential period at the Raymond Loewy Studios where he headed the Studebaker account, moved to Chrysler to spearhead their new 'Forward Look'. Exner, or rather Chrysler, was approached by Luigi Segre in 1951 with designs for a prototype Plymouth which was called the XX500. The prototype was built and this led to Segre and Exner penning a second design, the K-310. Exner's influence manifested itself in a deep swage line that ran down the lower part of the doors, before

The coupé was steadily refined too, and by the end of the decade had become a very elegant car. All it lacked was performance to match its looks.

In 1954 Karmann investigated the possibility of a four-seater Ghia coupé, and a pair of prototypes was built. However, the styling was clumsy and the project was shelved.

kicking up and over the rear wings. The side glass was rounded at the rear, and the windscreen sloped back at a steep angle. A second design, the Chrysler Coupé d'Elegance, had these features too.

A detailed plaster model of this second project was delivered to Turin at just about the same time as Ghia was struggling, it is said, with designs for the Karmann coupé. Exner claimed that Segre, stuck for inspiration, scaled down his design for the Coupé d'Elegance and turned it into the Karmann Ghia.

There are grounds for supporting Exner's claim. Although Ghia claimed to have toyed with the idea of a Volkswagen coupé as far back as 1950, why would a busy design studio spend its own time and money drawing up plans for such a car without a prior commission? And for what reason did Ghia insist on Karmann travelling to Paris to see the prototype, rather than Turin? Could it have been to ensure that Karmann didn't see the Exner design and draw his own conclusions?

Whatever the true story, the fact remains that the Karmann Ghia coupé was one of the most beautiful variations on the Beetle ever to see the light of day. That a company as conservative as Volkswagen (who else would dare to rely on one model for so long?) gave its blessing makes it all the more special.

HEBMÜLLER
THE FINEST OF THEM ALL?

In common with many other Karosseries, the Wuppertal-based company of Joseph Hebmüller and Sons had its roots firmly in coachbuilding. Founded in 1889, the company specialized in building horse-drawn carriages, and after Joseph's death in 1919 his four sons began to modify car bodies, opening a subsidiary operation in Wulfrath, Wuppertal. Among their customers were such names as Ford, Hanomag, Opel and Hansa-Lloyd, these companies being regular clients for many years to come. Hebmüller's specialities were two- and four-seater cabriolets and pullman saloons, primarily based on Ford or Opel chassis. Immediately after the Second World War, Hebmüller was commissioned by the British occupation forces to build fifteen special cabriolets on Humber chassis.

The 25,000th post-war Beetle rolled off the assembly line at Wolfsburg in May 1948. Under the

There can be few more elegant cars than the Hebmüller roadster. Unlike many other similar conversions, the Type 14A looks good from every angle.

guidance of Volkswagen's new leader, Heinz Nordhoff, plans were already being laid for the production of a cabriolet version of the Beetle. Following much discussion, two companies were chosen to see the project through. Karmann in Osnabrück would produce a five-seat cabriolet, Hebmüller a two-seat version. Both companies were advised to make use of as many saloon body parts as possible, and to retain the Beetle chassis and running gear in unmodified form.

Hebmüller built three prototypes in 1948, each based on very early cars. The tell-tale clue is the round

These three drawings show how Hebmüller's stylists wrestled with the lines – the two cabriolet models have very different roofs. A coupé was considered from the start.

jacking-point clearly seen in period photographs – this type of jacking point was only in use up until 1946. In each case, the original Beetle windscreen was retained, but the side windows were all-new and featured aluminium frames. Although at first it would appear that the rear engine cover was based on a front boot lid pressing, this was not the case. Each prototype was fitted with a hand-formed panel into which intake louvres were cut. The first car had four such louvres on either side of a central moulding, the other two had five. The numberplate light and single brake light were housed in a regular Beetle 'Pope's Nose' light

unit as fitted to all production VWs of the time.

Aside from the numbers of louvres, there were other differences between the first prototype and its successors. The original car was fitted with the 1946/47-style bumpers with banana over-riders, large VW-logo hubcaps, a dashboard-mounted rear-view mirror and a pair of large horns flush-mounted into the front wings – rather like the first cabrios produced after the war. A white three-spoked steering wheel was fitted, along with a radio, centrally-mounted aerial and a pair of large spotlights. This first car was finished in black.

Prototype No.1 dates back to 1948. Just discernible in this period photograph are the louvres in the rear lid. Note too the 'Pope's Nose' licence plate light.

Prototype No.2 was little different save for later bumpers and a very unusual set of hubcaps only ever seen on one other VW.

The second prototype was fitted with the later-style grooved bumpers with matching over-riders and came with a set of extremely unusual hubcaps of a design never seen again other than on the specially-built Beetle saloon destined for the Emperor of Abyssinia, which was displayed at the 1951 Frankfurt Motor Show. The interior mirror was relocated to the top of the windscreen, and like its predecessor, proto-type number two was painted black.

The third example was very similar, if not identical, to the second, the only detail differences being a grey paint finish, a chromium-plated numberplate light and later-style domed hubcaps.

The greatest problem that reared its head during testing was chassis flex. This resulted in poor door-alignment after just a few miles driving over the often badly-maintained roads of post-war Germany. Another serious problem that cropped up was that when the folding hood was being clipped into place on the windscreen surround the glass would often break as the surround flexed. These flexing problems

were solved with the first production Type 14A Hebmüller. The windscreen breakage was cured by incorporating a very heavy tubular frame into the wind-screen surround, this surround also being redesigned with somewhat more square corners. Inside the front luggage compartment a heavy steel plate can also be found, welded across the base of the windscreen.

The sills of the Hebmüller were also considerably strengthened by a long and heavy box-section pressing welded under each one, these incorporating the jacking points. Inside the car, the front bulkhead was reinforced by two panels welded in place alongside of the driver's and passenger's legs. The body was also strengthened in the rear. Extra side panels and strengthening plates were welded inside the car, with a large cross-member under the occasional rear seat. A pair of boxed reinforcing panels added rigidity to the engine bay, as well as housing the supports for the engine cover.

These improvements transformed the Hebmüller, and the first production test car built in April 1949

Life still went on almost as normal after the factory fire in July 1949, but the writing was on the wall. Here a string of new chassis is towed into the factory.

This view of the rear seat area of a Type 14A in for repair shows how much extra strengthening was used to retain rigidity.

The dashboards remained as per the saloon, but the kick panels were strengthened, as was the windscreen surround.

proved to be considerably more rigid than its predecessors. This example was subjected to some extreme tests, including being driven for some 10,000km over rough roads, and happily for the Hebmüller factory the redesigned cabriolet passed with flying colours. Following the successful conclusion of the test programme, full approval was granted by Wolfsburg and an order for 2000 vehicles received. Production began in June 1949 and the official title of Type 14A was granted.

Mechanically, the Type 14A was identical to the standard production Beetle, with mechanical brakes and a 25bhp engine.

There were a number of visual differences between the production version and the last of the prototypes, one of the more noticeable being the inclusion of a long scoop-like pressing in the engine lid that housed the numberplate light. At the same time, the air intake louvres were relocated from the engine lid to the rear deck, just ahead of the engine bay. Other external changes included fitting the same grooved aluminium trim as used on all export (deluxe) Beetles, as well as

two extra pieces, one on the engine lid, the other on the body between the intake louvres.

Despite jocular remarks to the effect that it was impossible to tell whether a Hebmüller was coming or going, one of the more appealing aspects of the design was its simple, uncluttered lines. With hood up or down, the Hebmüller cabriolet was a very attractive car. The whole roof could be folded away behind the occasional rear seat, and a tonneau cover fitted in its place. This could be carried out single-handed, as each side of the hood mechanism featured a spring-loaded damper that made the operation much easier.

The Hebmüller cabriolets were available in a variety of paint schemes, the two-tone designs being especially attractive. The most common single colours were black, red or white. As far as two-tone combina-

The factory at Wulfrath was a thriving operation in the late 1940s. In this photograph, it is possible to see how the regular saloon model was cut down to make the roadster.

In final production form, the Type 14A retained the trim used on the saloon models, but note that the semaphores are ahead of the doors – unlike the Karmann cabriolets.

tions were concerned, customers could choose from black and ivory, black and red, black and yellow or red and ivory. For an extra charge, customers could also specify a colour combination of their own choice.

The Hebmüllers were sold and serviced through the Volkswagen agencies on the domestic market, and elsewhere by private arrangement. The two-seater cabriolet sold well at a price of DM7500, and the future looked very bright for the company. All that was to change at around 14.00hrs on Saturday 23rd July 1949, when fire broke out in the paint spraying department, spreading rapidly through the rest of the paint shop and into some of the production area. The paint shop was completely destroyed and part of the factory roof collapsed onto machinery and partially-completed cars below. Was it sabotage, or an accident? No-one will ever know, but the question is how a factory caught fire on a Saturday afternoon.

After the fire was finally damped down, the damage was assessed. Things did not look as bad as had been first thought, and following a remarkable effort on the part of all concerned, the factory recommenced production just four weeks after the fire. At first output was rather slow, but in November 104 cars left the works, rising to 119 in December.

The start of the new decade saw 125 cabriolets leave in January, but it became apparent that Hebmüller had serious financial problems. Production fell to just 100 cars in February, 77 in March and a pitiful 17 in April. The end was in sight, for only one more vehicle (possibly for a different client) was produced at the Hebmüller factory, and that not until August of the following year.

The factory finally ground to a halt, and production of the Type 14A was transferred to the Karmann coachworks at nearby Osnabrück. In 1952, Hebmüller

registered itself bankrupt, having never fully recovered
from the effects of the fire. At Osnabrück a further
fifteen Type 14As were built before production finally
came to a close in 1953, when just one example was
built. It is not entirely clear how many were built as
the original production figure was given as 750, yet
only 696 are accounted for by official Volkswagen
records, which also list a breakdown by month:

1948	December	3	(Prototypes)
1949	April	1	(Production test car)
	June	27	(The start of production)
	July	28	
	August	24	
	September	17	
	October	39	
	November	104	
	December	119	
1950	January	125	
	February	100	
	March	77	
	April	17	
1951	August	1	
1952	May	12	(Now produced by Karmann)
	December	1	
1953	February	1	

Total Production   696

One of the most striking colour combinations has to be that of Bob Gilmore's car. Red over ivory was unusual but certainly attractive.

Engine access was improved as the whole of the rear deck of the car hinged out of the way.

Hebmüller prided itself on quality. Here, the finishing touches are added including hand-painting minor blemishes. Women worked alongside men at the factory.

The one and only coupé model ever built is believed to have been damaged beyond repair in an accident. The factory fire laid any further plans to rest.

Interior trim was to a higher standard than that usually found in Beetles. The extensive use of leather, along with neat styling touches, gave the Type 14A real class.

What is interesting to note, however, is that at least two vehicles exist today with body numbers above 700: one has the number 14 00705 (chassis number 10 148 544) and the other, 14 00710 (chassis number 10 149 314). The last chassis number recorded is for a 1952 example and is 10 344 735, but the body number is not known. From this it is possible to assume that, if body numbers were allocated in the order of production starting at 14 00000, then there were indeed in excess of 700 (at least 710, and possibly the 750 claimed by Hebmüller) Type 14As built. It is not so easy to guess production numbers from the chassis numbers as the chassis were obviously plucked from the production line at random.

So far all talk has been of cabriolets built at the Hebmüller works, but there was one – just one – coupé which also rolled out of the Wuppertal factory.

One year before production of the Type 14A commenced, the design for a 2+2 coupé was on the drawing board. By mid-1949 this design became a reality. It is unclear whether the vehicle in question was built entirely from scratch, or picked off the production line and converted, but there is one surviving photograph of the car and from it can be gleaned a few details.

The rear quarter windows could be hinged open, much like the later factory 'pop-out' windows, while

No less than fifty Type 14As await delivery outside the works. Two-tone paint was a popular choice, with black almost always the dominant colour.

the door glass retained its familiar aluminium surround, slightly modified at the rear edge to accommodate a vertical door post. From the rear view seen in the photograph, it is difficult to tell whether the windscreen of the cabriolet was retained, but judging from the angle of the windscreen pillar, it probably was.

Inside, it can only be surmised whether the rear seat was the same as on the cabriolet, but again, looking at the slope of the roof line, it is unlikely to have offered anything other than occasional accommodation.

But what became of the coupé? There are two stories, one being that it was sold, the other that it was written off in an accident with Paul Hebmüller at the wheel. It is quite possible that the former story came about after people had seen the similar Stoll coupé a few years later.

The Hebmüller remains one of the most attractive variations on the Beetle theme ever to see production. Today, over 100 examples are known to exist.

ROMETSCH
OF BEESKOW AND BANANAS

The coachbuilding concern of Friedrich Rometsch was founded in 1924 in Nestorstrasse, Berlin-Halensee. To begin with, the main source of income was from the construction of taxis, followed during the Second World War by somewhat unglamorous field kitchens. The taxis, built on Opel and Ley chassis towards the end of the 1920s, were magnificent vehicles, at once imposing yet elegant, and established Rometsch as a high-quality *Karosserie.*

In the post-war period, as the coachbuilding industry gradually began to re-establish itself, Rometsch, in common with many others, gratefully accepted commissions from a variety of clients. In 1950 an elegant cabriolet-bodied FIAT 1400 was displayed at a number of shows, while an unidentified but stunningly beautiful drophead coupé was completed at the Berlin works in 1951. Rometsch also began to consider the Volkswagen chassis for sporting models of its own.

However, taxis were to play an important part in

Rometsch's life for a long time to come. Late in 1951, a four-door Beetle taxi was announced, some 18cm/7in longer than a regular Beetle, yet just 25kg/55lb heavier. The increased length was much appreciated by fare-paying passengers who benefited from greatly increased legroom.

The plans for this model were drawn up by the talented Johannes Beeskow, who had already penned some designs for a sports cabriolet for Rometsch as far back as 1949. In order to carry out the necessary work, the Beetle first had to be completely dismantled, the whole conversion taking just a few weeks from start to finish. As might be expected, the most difficult aspect was the modification work needed to stretch the body and add an extra pair of doors. Work began by cutting across the roof behind the original doors, then a new panel was welded in place, exactly matching the complex contours of the existing sheet-metal. The new pillars for the rear doors were added next, supporting the new roof panel and giving the

Introduced in 1951, the Rometsch taxi was some 18cm/7in longer than a regular Beetle saloon. Note the extra pair of doors and the small rear side window. Rear-hinged rear doors gave easy access to the back seat.

The talented Johannes Beeskow was responsible for designing the Rometsch roadster, known by enthusiasts as the 'Banana' model because of its long, curving profile.

With hood up or down, the 'Banana' model is an extremely pretty car. The overall style is reminiscent of the Porsche 356 Speedster.

The front of the 'Banana' model looks rather blunt. Note the two-piece windscreen and heavy trim.

It was possible to carry a third passenger in a transverse occasional rear seat. When not in use, this folded away to give some extra luggage space.

The Rometsch was an elegant car from every angle. The substantial rear bumper offered more protection than was usually the case on Volkswagens.

whole structure some rigidity once again. The rear quarter panels were shortened, and a pair of new small side windows added. The front doors were also shortened, allowing larger rear doors to be fitted, thus improving access for passengers.

The chassis was cut and stretched by 22cms/8.6in, the extra material being turned up at the edges to give some strength to the join. The backbone was also reinforced, and all control cables, gear linkage, etc., lengthened to suit the new wheelbase.

The cost of the conversion was in the region of

DM2000, which did not include any of the other equipment – taximeter, lights, etc., – that a taxi-operator would require.

The four-door taxi was a successful vehicle for Rometsch, and many examples continued in use for several years. Its success could be measured in part by a report from the Vehicle Institute of the Berlin Technical University which, following the study of an example that had covered some 52,000km over an 18 month period, praised the suitability of the design for daily use as a taxi.

Yet praiseworthy as the taxi conversion might have been, there can be little doubt that it is the sports cabriolets that established Rometsch's reputation in Volkswagen circles. In 1950 Johannes Beeskow inspired Friedrich Rometsch to launch his first sports cabriolet, the model which became known as the 'banana' because of its long, curving shape. This basic design was used on many occasions by Beeskow. The FIAT 1400 of 1950, apart from the front grille, is very similar to his design for the Volkswagen-based cabriolet. Similarly, the Borgward Hansa 1500 coupé of 1952 was clearly from the same stable. Only the Goliath sports car of 1951/52 took on an altogether different form, this time resembling a Porsche 356 coupé.

The first public viewing of the Volkswagen-based cabriolet was at the 1950 Berlin Motor Show, and the response was sufficiently good for Rometsch to take the plunge and begin production the following year.

The banana model was available in either cabriolet or coupé forms, both models featuring a two-piece

In addition to a roadster, Rometsch also offered a coupé model (left). The first examples had small rear windows as seen here.

Later coupés (right) came with panoramic rear windows which gave considerably improved rear vision. Note the deep doors fitted to the 'Banana' model.

butted windscreen and wind-down side windows. The windscreen was supported on either side by pillars which formed part of the scuttle, being finished in body colour accordingly. Trim was kept to a minimum, with a simple polished metal strip along each flank and down the front and rear lids. Across the nose, and above the rear number plate, heavier chrome mouldings gave the otherwise relatively featureless body some form. The only other embellishments were raised 'eyebrows' above each front wheel-arch.

An intriguing aspect of the design was that the doors extended all the way down to the bottom of the sill. When the rear-hinged doors were opened, large strengthening members were revealed along each heater channel.

Unlike those fitted to the majority of special-bodied Beetles, the headlight units were not of Volkswagen origin, neither were the indicators or rear light assemblies. Instead, Rometsch sourced parts from a variety of suppliers to achieve the desired effect.

Mechanically, the banana model – or Beeskow, as it was also known – was Volkswagen Beetle through and through, but with the range of tuning options that became available during the 1950s few Rometschs remained in a low state of tune for long.

Inside both coupé and cabriolet, the seats were specially made to suit, and trimmed according to the customer's taste. Instrumentation was kept to the bare minimum, early models using the traditional split-window Beetle dashboard panels. Later the Rometsch came with its own dashboard layout which, while still relying on the Beetle for the basic instruments and controls, was unique to the model.

The dashboard of Blue Nelson's superb 1957 roadster shows the rare Rometsch steering wheel, ashtray, pull-out radio and Rometsch's own clock.

The two-tone paint of Nelson's car is unusual but very attractive. The roof is even trimmed in blue cloth.

One of the more intriguing aspects of the interior was the passenger accommodation. The backrests of the front seats could be tilted forward to gain access to a single rear seat that was fitted across the car. When not in use, the seat could be folded away and the space used for luggage. Immediately behind this third seat was a panel which opened to reveal more storage for soft baggage.

In 1954, the windscreen was changed for a one-piece curved design which instantly gave the Rometsch a more modern look while at the same time improving driver visibility. The rear window of the coupé was also considerably enlarged.

The Rometsch was not a small car, being some 4.40m/14ft 5in long and 1.58m/5ft 2in wide. Weight was in the region of 800kg/1760lb. Compared to a regular Export model Beetle at 4.07m/13ft 4in, 1.53m/5ft and 712kg/1568lb respectively, the Rometsch cabriolet was clearly a much larger vehicle all round than its Wolfsburg stablemate.

Such was the esteem in which the styling of the Beeskow cars was held that Rometschs were awarded a Golden Rose of Geneva in 1954, 1955 and 1956 for the quality of their coachwork.

In 1957, Friedrich Rometsch decided that it was time to redesign both the coupé and cabriolet models, the task being handled, not by Johannes Beeskow, but by Bert Lawrence from West Berlin. In retrospect, it may not have been a wise decision. The new design was notably different from the earlier model, considerable American influence being shown. The wrap-around windscreen, panoramic rear window and 'pinched' waist all gave the impression of the new Rometsch being a trans-Atlantic design. In almost all respects the new model had very little in common with its predecessor. The windscreen was now supported in an aluminium frame, while the body trim echoed that of the American Buick models, curving down across the doors before kicking back up and over the rear wheels.

At the rear, in place of the earlier individual units for indicator and tail lights, a larger single lens was fitted to the end of each wing. The cooling grille from a Porsche 356, set into the rear lid, allowed air into the engine bay.

The later model road-ster was nowhere near as attractive as the first cars. It was designed with the American market very much in mind.

Engine access was extremely good on all Rometschs thanks to a wide engine lid and long rear overhang.

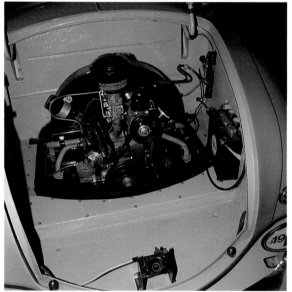

By now, more conventional front-hinged doors had been fitted, which no longer extended all the way to the lower edge of the sill panel. Also, the front luggage compartment, which housed the fuel tank as per normal Volkswagen practice, was much narrower than on the previous model.

Each vehicle took in the region of 1000 manhours to complete, with an aluminium body formed over a frame of steel and wood. The chassis and running gear remained original Volkswagen, but most of these later Rometschs were fitted with uprated Okrasa engines giving close to 50bhp, and a top speed of around 87mph/140kmh.

Inside the car, leather-trimmed bucket seats were fitted in the front, with Rometsch's characteristic transverse occasional seat behind. Instrumentation was again provided by the Beetle, but a matching clock was added alongside the speedometer.

At first only a cabriolet model was offered, but shortly afterwards it was joined by a coupé. Both were longer, wider and heavier than the original Beetle, as the earlier model had been, but the styling was not as widely acclaimed as Beeskow's banana design – despite winning another Golden Rose of Geneva award in 1957 – and consequently the new models never appeared to be as popular.

Rometsch introduced yet another variation in 1960, with less chrome trim, redesigned bumpers and a new look to the rear of the car. Although the effect was to make both coupé and cabriolet appear more elegant and sporting, the redesign did little to improve sales.

However, no matter what Friedrich Rometsch, Bert Lawrence or – had he not moved over to Karmann – Johannes Beeskow dreamed up for the Volkswagen-based sports cars, nothing could have prevented a political upheaval from virtually halving Rometsch's workforce overnight. On 13th August 1961 the infamous Berlin Wall was erected, at a stroke cutting the ancient capital city of Germany in two. Unfortunately, the majority of Rometsch's skilled labour lived in the eastern sector and could suddenly no longer travel to work. Rometsch had little option but to close its doors as a *Karosserie* in 1962.

Today Friedrich Rometsch lives on, though no longer as a coachbuilder of fine cabriolets and coupés.

DANNENHAUER & STAUSS
PERFECT IN EVERY WAY

Stuttgart is known as the home of one of the most exciting car manufacturers, Porsche, but back in the early 1950s it was also home to another company which specialized in producing roadsters powered by a rear-mounted air-cooled engine. That company was Dannenhauer & Stauss.

In the spring of 1950, Gottfried Dannenhauer and his son-in-law, Kurt Stauss, decided to set up a *Karosserie* in Augustenstrasse, Stuttgart. Dannenhauer had been an employee of Reutter, the company responsible for producing thirty of the Volkswagen prototypes (Porsche Type 60, or VW38) in 1937, and had learned many skills that would stand him in good stead.

Between them, Dannenhauer and Stauss felt confident of their abilities to build, trim and paint a sports cabriolet of their own design based, somewhat inevitably, on the Volkswagen chassis. However, when it came to design, the partners left the task in the hands of two of the most talented stylists in Germany

at the time: Herren Wagner and Oswald. These two men were well qualified to design a car body from scratch, having served under the influential and much-respected Professor Dr Wunibald Kamm of the Technical University of Stuttgart. Prof Dr Kamm was one of the pioneers of streamlining and is credited with being among the first in the world to recognize wind-tunnel testing as a vital element in the process of car design.

Wagner and Oswald began their partnership at Auto-Technik in Ueberlingen, at Lake Konstanz on the border with Switzerland. Here, in late 1949 and early 1950, they developed a two-seat sports cabriolet based on the Volkswagen which sold for DM3500. As far as is known, only one example was ever built,

Dannenhauer & Stauss No.1. The simple and very pleasing lines remained little changed throughout the D&S's life. Note the suicide doors and semaphore indicators.

The Auto-Technik was the forerunner of the Dannenhauer & Stauss, also designed by Wagner and Oswald. Only one example is thought to have been built.

Version No.2 was this roadster. Note the two-piece windscreen, suicide doors and lack of semaphores. This 1950 car survives.

although the services of their *Karosserie* were advertised in a contemporary publication, *Das Auto Motor und Sport*. It was this experience with the Auto-Technik that made Wagner and Oswald eminently suitable for the task of creating a VW-based roadster.

In common with many special-bodied cars of the era, the finished design resembled a Porsche 356 from certain angles, notably the side and the front. However, the Dannenhauer & Stauss prototype, being based on the standard Volkswagen chassis, sat higher than the Porsche, which had by now forsaken a separate floorpan in favour of unitary construction.

The chassis for the prototype was purchased minus body from the local Volkswagen agent. As was so often the case, chassis supply was to prove a major headache throughout the Dannenhauer & Stauss's life. A few were bought from Hahn, the Stuttgart VW agency, others from Mahag in Munich, Schultz in Düsseldorf and Essen, Krauss in Nürnberg, Glinicke in

Kassel, Graber in Switzerland and even Scania Vabis in Sweden! The remainder were either supplied by customers, or – as in at least five instances – built up from individual parts. It was not until early in 1955 that Wolfsburg relented and made a few bare chassis available.

Unlike many similar vehicles, the Dannenhauer & Stauss featured a body formed from steel. To begin, a full-size wooden buck was made, over which each section of the body was hammered from various thicknesses of steel, ranging from 0.8mm to 1.0mm. All the individual sections were then welded together to make the body. In all, six sections made up the front wings, while the rears were made from eight separate parts! Only the door skins, engine cover and front lid were made from single panels, although of double-skinned construction. The windscreen of the prototype, in common with some early production versions, was a two-piece butted design, rather like that of the first

This 1953 Dannenhauer & Stauss is a very attractive little car. Porsche-style wheels were a popular addition.

Later cars can be identified from the rear by the slim intake grille on the engine cover. Note the later-style bumpers too.

Porsches. In detail, however, no two Dannenhauer & Stauss cars were every exactly the same, thanks to the hand-built nature of the product.

The doors were rear-hinged, early models using Volkswagen handles on the exterior, later (post-1954) examples using Porsche 356 handles. Unlike the Auto-Technik that preceded it, the Dannenhauer & Stauss's door hinges were hidden from view. Also unlike the Auto-Technik, the rear deck area of the car was rela-

tively short, giving the impression of the car sitting back on its haunches ready to spring into action. The Auto-Technik, incidentally, owed its long rear end to a lockable luggage compartment between the engine lid and the back edge of the cockpit, accessible only from outside the car.

The Dannenhauer & Stauss prototype was relatively free from excessive adornment. On each side a trim strip ran along the sill panel, and another rearward

The dashboard on early models clearly echoed that of the split-window Beetle. Note the accessory radio.

As the Beetle was updated, so was the Dannenhauer & Stauss. When the saloon dashboard changed in 1952, so did the D&S.

from the windscreen pillars. Across the front panel two small pieces of trim could be found, while another ran along the centre of the bonnet. In fact, throughout the Dannenhauer & Stauss's life simplicity of linc was a trademark, with a streamlined overall shape with bolt-on rear wings.

The interior was designed and trimmed by Dannenhauer & Stauss because there were no suitable Volkswagen seats available. The lower seating position dictated by the low roof line necessitated new seats on narrower runners, and these were normally trimmed in imitation leather, although customers who were prepared to pay an extra DM350 could specify the real thing.

The rear seat provided accommodation for two adults or three small children, and comprised a pair of sparsely-padded wooden boards. The backrest hinged forward to allow access to luggage space behind the occupants. For an extra DM39 it was possible to order a luxury version of the rear seat with extra padding and a sprung base.

The folding hood was a very professional-looking affair, stuffed with horsehair to give it both strength and form. Inside, a full headlining was fitted, much like that of the Karmann cabriolet. Early models had a small wooden-framed rear window which allowed the driver a limited view of the road behind, while later examples had a sewn-in plastic window.

103

This D&S coupé was built to order in 1954 for a wealthy tobacco dealer in Wiesbaden. It featured a Porsche engine and brakes.

For the 1953 model year a single-piece curved windscreen was used which gave the Dannenhuer & Stauss a more modern look. The overall styling was also revised.

A small number – possibly only three, no one is entirely certain – of coupé versions were built, making the little car very much an all-weather vehicle. The coupé featured a wide, panoramic rear window and wind-up side windows for the front and rear passengers, very much like the Karmann cabriolet. It was therefore possible to drive with all side windows wound down out of view.

The first of these coupés was discussed in *Das Auto Motor und Sport*, in which a Herr Wehr wrote, 'Now, for the first time, he [Dannenhauer] has also built a well-proportioned and attractive coupé'. The car was finished in black with an interior in pastel green and beige. The second coupé was built some time during 1953, being delivered with two-tone paintwork,

whitewall tyres and a standard 30bhp engine.

However, the third coupé that is known to have existed was a somewhat more potent vehicle. Ordered in 1954 by a wealthy cigar and tobacco dealer in Wiesbaden, the coupé was ultimately fitted with a Porsche engine and brakes which must have given the Dannenhauer & Stauss the performance its looks deserved.

The dashboard of all models at first very strongly echoed the design of the split-window Beetle's, with a pair of small glove boxes positioned either side of two instrument panels. The left-hand panel housed the speedometer, the right-hand one either a clock or a radio (or even a combination of the two), according to choice. Towards the end of 1951 the design changed,

Kurt Stauss is still to be found at the Augustenstrasse workshops, but is no longer involved in producing special-bodied Volkswagens.

with a single, central radio panel, very much along the lines of that used in contemporary Porsches. When Volkswagen redesigned the dashboard of the Beetle in 1953, Dannenhauer & Stauss followed suit, making use of the new radio blanking plate, central grille and new-style speedometer.

In keeping with the introduction by Volkswagen of new bumpers in October 1952, Dannenhauer & Stauss updated its design to suit. However, this was not just an enforced changeover from the early grooved bumpers, but was instead seen as an opportunity to mildly redesign the car. The front end was extended by something over 5cms/2in, while the rear was stretched approximately 2cms/0.8in. This subtle change gave the cabriolet a smoother, more aerodynamic appearance, further enhanced by mounting the bumpers at a slightly lower level but retaining the small closing panel between each bumper and valance – a feature common to all Dannenhauer & Stauss cars.

At the same time the rear of the car was updated, the characteristic (and somewhat Hebmüller-like) long central moulding being discarded in favour of a simple grille not at all dissimilar to that used on a Porsche 356. This grille was the sole source of air for the engine cooling system. At first these were made at the Augustenstrasse workshops, but from January 1953 they were supplied by Graeppel. Porsche provide the chrome-plated numberplate light which incorporated

the Dannenhauer & Stauss's only brake light.

The most significant change was the incorporation of a single, curved windscreen in place of the original two-piece design. Although this did much to improve the appearance of the cabriolet, the cost of each individual car was increased considerably.

One interesting point is that, from the outset, flashing indicators were fitted to the cars, initially only at the rear, but later at the front too. Semaphore indicators were retained on many models, although there was no hard and fast rule concerning this. Headlight units were from a Beetle, whereas the rear-light units were made by Hella and could also be found on early Porsche 356s, DKWs and others.

Each car generally left the *Karosserie* with a standard Volkswagen engine, at first the modest 25bhp version, then the more practical 30bhp unit, but some customers felt that the sporting looks of the Dannenhauer & Stauss deserved better, uprating their engines with a kit from Okrasa. Kurt Stauss also recalls some customers fitting the Swiss-made MAG supercharger in the search for more power. Fitting the twin-carburettor Okrasa engine presented few problems due to the greatly-increased width of the engine bay, but when a standard engine was specified the air-filter assembly had to be relocated behind the fan-housing as the low line of the engine lid prevented it from being fitted in the original position.

The engine bay of the Dannenhauer & Stauss allows easy access for the mechanic. Note the relocated air-filter necessitated by the lower body line.

Fitting an Okrasa engine was a popular pastime in the fifties. With its wide engine bay, the D&S lends itself well to the twin carburettor conversion.

As the finished vehicles weighed in the region of 778kg/1715lb, the acceleration with a standard Beetle engine was leisurely rather than sporting. However, the improved aerodynamics helped to increase the top speed slightly. Early cars were available with raised compression and a 32mm Solex carburettor fitted to an otherwise standard 1131cc engine. Power was thus increased to over 34bhp, resulting in a top speed in excess of 70mph.

When first introduced in 1951, the Dannenhauer

& Stauss cabriolet body (less chassis and engine) cost DM4250. By the time production came to an end in 1956, the cost had risen to DM5342, with the chassis costing an additional DM3400. Certain extras could also be specified, including a steering lock (DM34), as well as the luxury rear seats (DM39) and leather upholstery (DM350) already mentioned. When the last example rolled out of the workshops at a total price of DM8742 including taxes, the Standard Beetle cost DM3790, while an Export (De Luxe) version cost

DM4600. The Karmann cabriolet cost only DM5990, – and could seat four in comfort. The Ghia coupé when it was introduced late in 1957 was priced at just DM8250. By comparison, the Dannenhauer & Stauss was too expensive and ultimately this would prove to be its downfall.

Kurt Stauss can still be found in the same Augustenstrasse premises, but sadly no longer concerned with the production of limited-edition special-bodied Volkswagens. Instead the business – now run by his daughter Gisela – concentrates on body repair, a far more lucrative market.

Nobody has any accurate idea of how many Dannenhauer & Stauss cabrios were made, not even Herr Stauss himself. He prefers not to guess, feeling that such games benefit no one, but guesswork on the part of enthusiasts puts the figure at something

Andy Luzzi's roadster viewed from this unusual angle shows off its simple yet aesthetically pleasing lines. Only the bolt-on rear wings date the car.

between 80 and 135. Herr Stauss does recall that each car took between 800 and 1000 hours to complete. He rarely got to meet the owners of the cars as they were almost always ordered through dealers and sadly, as no files were kept ('Creating files doesn't pay any money', he says), no record of customers, or vehicle specification, exists.

Today, there are just sixteen known survivors in the world, none of them coupés.

BEUTLER
VANS, WAGONS AND STUNNING COUPÉS

The first Beutler Volkswagens lacked the style of their later counterparts, with simple lines and modest trim. This model was first seen in 1954.

Founded later than many other well-known coach-builders, in 1946, the Swiss family concern of Ernst Beutler was responsible for producing some of the most stylish special-bodied Volkswagens ever seen. The first Beutler versions of the Volkswagen Beetle were what came to be known as 'Utes' – utility vehicles. They were pick-up models built in reasonable numbers, achieving peak popularity between 1950 and 1952. Sadly, it is believed that none of these early conversions have survived.

In March 1949 the company, located at 40-42 Gwattstrasse, Thun-Dürrenmat in the Canton of Bern, displayed a prototype body for the recently-released Porsche 356 at the Geneva Motor show. Without doubt, the Beutler 356 and the original factory coupé together stole the show.

Built as a joint venture between Beutler, Porsche – then located at Gmünd – and the Swiss company of Blank Automobil of Zurich, the Beutler Porsche was typical of the time with its two-piece, butted wind-screen, aluminium body on a steel frame and a folding convertible roof. In all, six of these models had been ordered by the close of the Geneva show, one of

which was to be fitted with an occasional rear seat at the request of the customer.

When Porsche made the move from Gmünd to the famous Stuttgart works, it decided to review the whole situation regarding special-bodied cars. The result of this was that Beutler lost its right to build any more special 356s, leaving the way open for Reutter to expand on its relationship as Porsche's chosen body-builder.

In common with all Porsches of the time, the Beutler variations retained much that could be identi-fied as having originated at Wolfsburg. The engines were extensively reworked 25bhp Beetle units, with twin carburettors, special cylinder heads with canted valves and a reduced capacity of 1086cc (achieved by using smaller cylinders of 73.5mm instead of 75mm

The later Beutlers were far more attractive. Side trim is reminiscent of the later Type 3 Karmann Ghia, and other than badging there was nothing to distinguish the Beutler-Porsche from the Beutler-VW. The grille is very like that of the Mercedes 300SL.

The so-called US model featured a wider grille. This Porsche-engined version (above and left) has been fitted with wheels and intake grilles from the 356 Porsche.

This car belonging to Alain Vuilleumier is a 1954 model, chassis number 1-0 731 322, and is equipped with a Porsche Super 75 engine.

The interior does little to betray the Volkswagen origins. Instrumentation and trim are more what one would associate with a Porsche.

bore). The result of these modifications was to increase power output to 40bhp at 4200rpm – a far cry for the Beetle's 25bhp at 3000rpm – and torque from 6.74mkg (49.0lb.ft) at 2000rpm to 7.15mkg (51.9lb.ft) at 2800rpm. This was enough to propel the tiny two-seater to an impressive maximum speed of around 87mph/140kmh.

The basic Beetle, albeit in the better-equipped export form, had made its first official appearance in Switzerland through the efforts of AMAG (Automobil and Motoren Aktien-Gesellschaft, the VW importer) in May 1948. The car soon became extremely popular

with the Swiss and it was not long before Beutler began to take a look at the possibilities offered by the VW's platform chassis.

First of all, though, in the following year, Beutler displayed a Beetle with the extremely advanced feature of a plexiglass roof panel that could be opened at the rear edge to allow the through-flow of air. In fact, if so required, the whole roof panel could be removed completely to give true open-air motoring. Although the concept of a tilting or removable roof panel is commonplace today, in 1949 the idea was viewed with a degree of awe. It is believed that a total of

During restoration the bodywork was stripped back to bare metal, allowing us to appreciate the fine workmanship.

twelve of these Beutler Beetles were built, but they have paled into insignificance alongside the more exotic-looking coupés that began to fill Beutler's life from that point on.

In 1954, once again at the Geneva Motor Show, Beutler showed its new sports car based on the Volkswagen chassis. The car, displayed in both coupé and cabriolet styles, was an elegant design with a longer, lower appearance than that of the contemporary Porsche 356. Unusually, the coupé version was considered to be better looking than the cabriolet – a reversal of normal thinking.

The front of the two models featured what became Beutler's trademark, a fake grille which bore more than a passing resemblance to that of the 300SL Mercedes-Benz, but the remainder of the body was free of trim other than a single spear running along the sill panel below the door on each side.

The problem of chassis supply was overcome with the assistance of the nearby Moser Garage, an official Volkswagen dealership in Thun which still operates today. This garage even went so far as to offer servicing and marketing facilities to Beutler.

Designed by Ernst Beutler, and built over a three-month period under the supervision of his brother, the coupés were produced to order. These Beutlers captured the public imagination at a time when there was much debate over what the 'car of the future' might look like. Many styling exercises – especially those in America – took on outlandish forms that would clearly never make it into production. The

Beutler, however, achieved a balance between practicality and stylish good looks that made it a far more feasible proposition.

From the outset the car was offered in either coupé or cabriolet form, with a hardtop version available to order. The basic construction was similar on all vehicles, with a hand-formed aluminium body bolted onto the Beetle floorpan. The use of stressed bulkheads gave the body a great deal of rigidity, making the cabriolet model far less susceptible to scuttle shake than other similar cars.

The doors on all models were built without window frames and were very generous in their proportions, allowing easy access to both front and rear seats. The interior was well-appointed and featured seats specially made by Beutler which were available trimmed in either cloth or imitation leather. The rear seat could be folded forward in two sections to afford extra luggage space when needed. A cloth headlining was fitted to all models.

Unless otherwise specified, the instrumentation was that of a Beetle, with just the basic speedometer providing the information. However, Beutler did see fit to add an oil temperature gauge and fuel gauge too, along with a cigarette lighter and an aftermarket – usually Petri – steering wheel with horn ring.

Mechanically, these vehicles were offered with the standard Volkswagen engine (referred to as Beutler-

111

For use by the factory, Beutler built this pick-up, seen here awaiting restoration. It was a crude conversion, possibly of a car that had been damaged. At **the rear all the original panels remained in place. The upper parts were simply sliced off to accept the pick-up bed.**

VWs), but some versions were available with the Porsche 356 engine and braking system, giving rise to their being termed Beutler-Porsches. The early Beutler-Porsche was one of those rare vehicles that had official blessing from Stuttgart to carry the Porsche badge front and rear. It is unclear, but it is believed that the Porsche version was only available between 1954 and 1956.

The coupé design was updated in 1957, at which time it took on the appearance of a very svelte sports car that looked distinctly more exotic than its humble Volkswagen underpinnings would otherwise suggest. Two versions of the coupé were available, a European model with small front grille, and a so-called US model which featured a wider grille and finned rear wings. The lines were stretched slightly, and updated with less pronounced rear wings and revised body trim. It is interesting to note that the rear wings of some examples featured trim that very closely resembled that which would be fitted by Karmann to its Type 3-based Ghia coupé in 1962.

The handling of the Beutler coupé was far superior to that of the Beetle, thanks in part to the lower centre of gravity, which was helped by relocating the fuel tank further forward and lower down than in a Beetle. Although the coupé version weighed in at some 50kg more than a Beetle, the acceleration and top speed could be improved by the addition of Beutler's own twin carburettor conversion. A top speed of around 87mph/140kmh was possible with this modification, and with the availability of Okrasa and Denzel conversions, or the fitment of a MAG or Judson supercharger, the customer could choose his own method of further increasing performance. Those who chose to order a Beutler-Porsche could, in theory at least, have specified anything up to and including the mighty Carrera four-cam motor, although it appears that nobody took advantage of that course of action!

Cost was always a problem with special-bodied cars like the Beutler, more so since Volkswagen's own Karmann Ghia coupé benefited from factory support that resulted in a more competitive price structure. Too often, what were essentially little more than basic Beetles fitted with another bodyshell proved to be almost as costly (in Beutler's case at some 21,900 Swiss

One of Beutler's first vehicles was this useful station wagon which appeared in the early 1950s. This well-executed conversion was available until the end of the decade.

Alongside the station wagon was this van with roll-down sides. The biggest drawback was the lack of load area. Note the use of Beetle rear lights turned sideways on the rear quarters.

Francs) as the far more exciting Porsche 356.

Realizing that there was possibly an opening in the market for a Porsche with family appeal, Beutler acquired a Porsche 356B from Stuttgart and produced a 2+2 coupé body on the unitary chassis. The prototype was displayed at the 1959 Geneva Motor show, where both Porsche and Beutler watched public reaction with interest. It seems that neither felt the response sufficiently overwhelming to consider production.

There were other Beutler-VWs available during the 1950s, these being the van conversions that transformed the Beetle into a useful delivery wagon with

roll-down sides. There was also a station wagon version with long side windows for the family man.

On the van the cooling air for the engine was drawn in via louvres stamped into the curved engine lid, whereas the station wagon – which featured a large opening tailgate – drew breath through cooling vents set high up on the rear quarters in similar fashion to the Type 2 models of the 1970s.

Both versions made use of Beetle tail lights fitted to the rear quarters in line with the tops of the rear wings – the light units were turned through 90°, but were otherwise unmodified. The original Beetle rear bumper was also fitted, this looking strangely out of

place on the station wagon's squared-off tail.

One of the drawbacks as far as the station wagon was concerned was the length of time it took to convert from a four-seater into a load-carrier. First you had to fold down the rear seat backrest, then screw into place a tubular frame and finally slot into position some plywood flooring. This was locked into place with quarter-turn fasteners. The procedure was made all the more inconvenient by the fact that the extra flooring could not be carried inside the vehicle while it was being used as a four-seater.

Even with the new floor in position there was little to be gained. Thanks to the rear engine location the floor ended up being at shoulder level to the driver, meaning that the loading area was a scant 60cm/24in high – little use to anyone who wanted to carry anything more bulky than a set of golf clubs.

Engine accessibility suffered, too, with the original engine bay being retained intact, despite the roomier appearance given by the apparently voluminous rear bodywork. Indeed, on opening the engine lid the owner was confronted by the standard Beetle rear valance, rear wings and bulkhead. The Beutler conversion was virtually 'slipped over' the original Beetle bodywork! As a consequence, the engine was

Although not a common sight, Beutlers do appear for sale now and then, This example was on offer by a Swiss garage in 1992.

difficult to work on, space being so tight that a remote-mounted Karmann Ghia air-filter had to be fitted.

Neither conversion was as popular as might have been expected, for both should have made ideal vehicles for small businessmen such as greengrocers, bakers, etc. The vehicles' downfall was once again cost, as Volkswagen's own larger Type 2 model offered considerably more accommodation for little extra money.

The majority of Beutler's products have long since disappeared, although the pick-up built by the company for its own use has survived and is due to be restored soon. A few coupés are known to survive. One example was offered for sale in Switzerland in 1992 by a dealer following an apparently recent restoration. Lacking much of its original trim, the coupé was offered at a price that would have bought a very nice Porsche 356. Some things never change...

WAIFS & STRAYS
THE PLIGHT OF THE HOMELESS

As we have seen, there were many special-bodied versions of the Volkswagen Beetle, built by everyone from the Wolfsburg factory down to the backyard mechanic. We are fortunate that a large percentage of these have been documented in one way or another, even if only to tell us the name of the person who built them and maybe even when, but there are also many cars clearly based on the ubiquitous Beetle about which we know little or nothing at all. All that remains in some cases is a faded photograph of a long-forgotten car, with only a tell-tale badge to betray a Volkswagen connection. Hopefully the publication of this book will help flush out more information on these and other as yet undiscovered coachbuilt or cabriolet Beetles.

Another unknown that surfaced at a swap meeting in the USA. Nobody knows who was responsible for this coupé, but whoever it was, they knew what they were doing.

Who built this roadster? It looks rather like the Auto-Technik (see Chapter 11), but clearly isn't the same car. Nipple hubcaps suggest a very early chassis.

The stylist really went to town on this station wagon, a very professionally done conversion. Note the two-piece windscreen, restyled rear wings and fake grille. Only the hubcaps betray the origins.

An Italian company was responsible for producing this minibus. Once again, only the hubcaps give away the fact that this was yet another VW-based conversion.

From the sublime to the ridiculous: this space-age creation resembles a flying saucer more than a Beetle. It was based on parts from both a Porsche 356 and a Beetle.

Only the familiar VW badge gives the game away, but you would never know otherwise that this saloon car is based on Beetle components. Or is it?

The 1954 Spohn was one of the first cars to be built using glassfibre as a body material. Little else is known, and certainly none survive.

California collector Blue Nelson recently acquired this special. The rear end is from a Karmann Ghia, the front end from parts of a Porsche 550 Spyder.

The Tempo-Matado was a front-engined commercial vehicle available as a pick-up, van or bus. An interesting deviation from the rear-engined theme.

The lines are reminiscent of the Kubinsky roadster (Chapter 6), but the curved windscreen is far more modern. And who is the proud owner sat behind the wheel?

This Porsche-like creation was built in Czechoslovakia sometime, presumably, in the 1960s. Little is known about the car other than that it is based on early running gear.

Another extremely professional conversion, but by whom, and when? Again, only the hubcaps show that this is a Volkswagen-based vehicle. Very interesting.

LOST & FOUND
DISCOVERIES AND PROJECTS

Every restoration begins with an unrestored car. Some need little more than a repaint and retrim, others need somewhat more. Take a look at this selection of diamonds in the dust and remember – it pays to keep your eyes open wherever you go. You never know what you might find down in the woods.

Enough to make you cry. This V8-engined roadster, based on a 1949 Hebmüller, was raced and then finally scrapped.

Looking slightly lost without its wings, this Hebmüller has at least been saved.

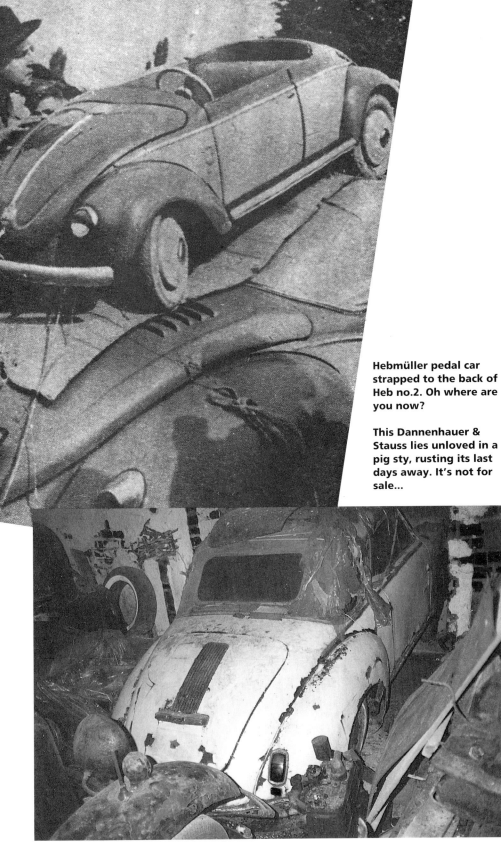

Hebmüller pedal car strapped to the back of Heb no.2. Oh where are you now?

This Dannenhauer & Stauss lies unloved in a pig sty, rusting its last days away. It's not for sale...

The bumper's right, the lights are wrong, but underneath it's still a Heb.

A Dannenhauer & Stauss found in Sweden. Fortunately this one was kept covered up.

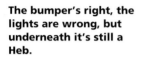

Hard frontal damage, but that won't deter Blue Nelson from restoring this Rometsch.

122

A different kind of Hebmüller – this Type 18A police car needs plenty of TLC.

Bob Shaill proudly poses with his Heb – discovered on waste-land in South London c1980.

Bob's Stoll coupé on the left and, unbelievably, the same Heb on the right.

The bumpers are wrong, and so are the rear lights, but the rest of this Heb is all there...

1952 Karmann cabriolet discovered in woodland in Finland, parked there since 1965.

1953 Dannenhauer & Stauss looking forward to the day when restoration begins at last.

'Cal Look' Denzel? Empi wheels and a hot Volkswagen engine give a Denzel a new look.

A rare Tuscher roll-back roof model with restoration well under way.

'Hollywood Ralph'
c1980. A hoarder rather
than a restorer, sad to
say, here with a D&S.

Down on the
farm...Apart from the
wings and bumpers,
this Heb doesn't look
too bad.

It's all there and ripe for
restoration. This
Rometsch 'Banana'
went to a good home.

The one and only Waibel awaits restoration. Check out those fender skirts!

Not a lot wrong with this Beutler at first sight, but closer examination revealed a lot of rust in the floors.

Just to prove that the effort is all worthwhile. One of Blue Nelson's Rometschs enjoys the summer sun.